CALLED TO SERVE

A THEOLOGY OF COMMISSIONED MINISTRY

DAVID L. RUETER

CONCORDIA PUBLISHING HOUSE · SAINT LOUIS

Founded in 1869 as the publishing arm of The Lutheran Church—Missouri Synod, Concordia Publishing House gives all glory to God for the blessing of 150 years of opportunities to provide resources that are faithful to the Holy Scriptures and the Lutheran Confessions.

Published by Concordia Publishing House
3558 S. Jefferson Ave., St. Louis, MO 63118-3968
1-800-325-3040 • www.cph.org

Cover: Kees Zwanenburg/ShutterStock

Manufactured in the United States of America

LIBRARY OF CONGRESS CATALOGING-IN-PUBLICATION DATA

Names: Rueter, David L., author.
Title: Called to serve : a theology of commissioned ministry / David L. Rueter.
Description: St. Louis, MO : Concordia Publishing House, [2019] | Includes bibliographical references and index.
Identifiers: LCCN 2018058900 (print) | LCCN 2019000092 (ebook) | ISBN 9780758662514 (ebook) | ISBN 9780758662521 (print)
Subjects: LCSH: Lutheran Church--Missouri Synod. | Lutheran Church--Missouri. | Lay ministry--Lutheran Church--History. | Pastoral theology--Lutheran Church--History.
Classification: LCC BX8061.M7 (ebook) | LCC BX8061.M7 R83 2019 (print) | DDC 262/.1441322--dc23
LC record available at https://lccn.loc.gov/2018058900

1 2 3 4 5 6 7 8 9 10 28 27 26 25 24 23 22 21 20 19

Contents

Acknowledgments

Thank you to my parents, Roger and Nancy, for their ministry as Lutheran teachers and the vision for ministry formed in me through their faithful service and whose modeling of what it means to be church workers set a foundation for my life.

Many thanks to my colleagues at Concordia University Irvine. Especially Rev. Dr. Steve Mueller for encouraging my application to the Trembath Chair of Confessional Theology that allowed for the research for this book. Thanks also to my colleagues Dr. Joel Oesch, Dr. Dan Dean, Rev. Dr. Glenn Fluege, and Rev. Dr. David Loy for their feedback during the development of this work. Additionally, I want to thank my partner in the DCE Program, Prof. Rebecca Duport for her support and excellent work with our students, especially during my absence for this research, as well as to our students in the DCE program who put up with my being less available.

Thank you also to Dr. Jim McConnell and Dr. Steve Christopher for their shaping my formation as a DCE. To all the DCEs with whom I have served in the Pacific Southwest District, thank you for always being a fantastic group to serve alongside. Thank you to the staff of the Pacific Southwest District, especially Rachel Klitzing and Rev. Dr. Larry Stoterau, for your support and encouragement.

Finally, most especially I want to thank my wife, Andrea, for her support, as well as my boys, James and Wesley, for their excitement that their dad was writing another book. Most of all to my Savior Jesus Christ, in whose name I seek to serve the Church in truth and faithfulness.

ABBREVIATIONS	
AC	Augsburg Confession
Ap	Apology of the Augsburg Confession
LW	Luther's Works
SD	Solid Declaration of the Formula of Concord

Preface

My parents met in high school in Santa Ana. Both responded to the call to serve as Lutheran school teachers. When she was not fulfilling her vocation as a stay-at-home mom, my mother taught first and/or second grade. My father was for most of his career a principal, teaching as called for based on the size of the Lutheran schools where he served. He was even my principal for ten years. The final two of those years, he was not only my principal but also my seventh and eighth grade teacher. For a time, my sister also served as a Lutheran school teacher.

In high school, my close group of friends came from three local Lutheran churches (an interesting feat considering I attended a high school associated with the Christian Reformed Church and Reformed Church of America). We regularly rotated from one church's youth group to the next. The three youth groups became so intertwined that, years later, discussions have arisen about which church various participants actually belonged to.

Two of these churches had a Director of Christian Education (DCE) responsible for youth ministry, among other areas of ministry (Jim and Brad). My own home church did not have a DCE to serve in ministry alongside the pastor, but these two other churches did, which gave me a window into another form of church work. Getting to know both of these very different men was eye opening for me. Both took particular interest in my formation. Both found ways to not only engage me in the life of their churches beyond youth group, but also prepared me for leadership in those groups.

Following graduation, I enrolled at Christ College Irvine (now Concordia University Irvine). Hedging my bets, I at first registered as a double major in both accounting and religious studies. I had worked for the father of a friend of mine during high school, who was a tax preparer, specializing in taxes for church workers. My theory was that taking the religious studies major would allow me to become a DCE like Jim and Brad, while the accounting major might be a safer bet financially, just in case I did not make it in ministry. It took my first tax accounting class but also interacted with students in the DCE program as well as Dr. Steve Christopher, the director of the program. Those interactions convinced me that my home was in the DCE program. My vocational calling was to DCE ministry.

Now, twenty years later, I sit in my office (in the building that once housed my freshman dorm room) as a professor for the DCE program, as Steve once was. The years of ministry as a DCE in both Texas (internship) and Southern California have confirmed my calling into DCE ministry.

However, along the way, I have had times in which I have questioned that calling. I have encountered—either in books, articles, or podcasts—well-meaning Lutheran theologians and pastors whose understanding of ministry caused me to question my own. What does it mean when I use the phrase "DCE ministry"? Is "ministry" properly something done only by pastors? Or are DCEs, Lutheran teachers, Directors of Christian Outreach (DCO), deaconesses, Directors of Parish Music (DPM), Lay Ministers, or Directors of Family Life Ministry (DFLM) in ministry as well?[1] If these commissioned ministers are in fact in some way in ministry, how does their ministry relate to the Office of the Public Ministry? Are their offices "public" as well?

From the beginning of The Lutheran Church—Missouri Synod (LCMS), both pastors and teachers have been members of the synod.[2] Both have had specific and rigorous training provided for them. Both have been called by congregations and affiliated schools. Yet despite the long history of the called Lutheran teacher as a worker in the LCMS, pastors have been the only church workers who have been granted voting rights in district and synodical conventions.[3]

In order to achieve a well-balanced approach to ecclesiastical governance, each congregation is granted one pastoral delegate and one lay delegate for district conventions. A similar arrangement, built upon a district's electoral circuits, provides pastoral and lay delegates to synodical conventions. Commissioned ministers like myself have no vote at either. At district conventions, commissioned ministers are expected only to attend and are able to speak in floor committees and on the convention floor. At synodical conventions, a group of advisory delegates are sent by each district's commissioned ministers in proportion to the number of commissioned ministers in the district. Again, they are able to speak on the floor of the convention, but having seen this in action, it tends to be rather challenging to get the opportunity to do so from the back of the room. Commissioned ministers are represented on various boards and commissions of the synod and districts and do serve on convention floor committees. In this way, there is at least some representation in the governance of the synod.

Since my current call is to both Concordia University Irvine and the Pacific Southwest District, I find myself in an even more unique position. I also serve my congregation in ways not defined by my current DCE call: teaching Bible

---

1 This list of offices is taken from Article V.B of the current LCMS Constitution. Item 11 on the list, certified Lay Ministers, refers to rostered church workers like those prepared at Concordia University Wisconsin.

2 Congregations are members of the synod as are rostered workers. Individual laity are members of their congregation, but they are not members of the synod in the same way that a congregation or a rostered worker is. For more specifics, see https://www.lcms.org/handbook.

3 Meyer, Carl S. *Moving Frontiers,* 150.

class, assisting with youth ministry, and serving as an elder.[4] Almost any other member of the congregation who serves in these voluntary ministry roles would be eligible to represent the church in convention. However, due to my status as a called worker, I am ineligible to serve as a voting delegate and represent my congregation. Likewise, the many ordained and commissioned colleagues with whom I teach at Concordia University Irvine have been determined to be ineligible to serve as voting delegates at both district and synodical conventions.

Setting aside the question of voting, the complexity of this issue remains. My call to both train future church workers and to support current district workers has led me to see the need to study this at greater depth. Whenever there is a discussion of ministry or specifically the Office of the Public Ministry, my ears perk up. I have a stake in understanding the varying positions that have developed in the LCMS over the years since our founding in 1847.

Sutton explains what it means to be a Lutheran, discussing the Office of the Public Ministry and its relationship to the Priesthood of All Believers.[5] What for most would seem straightforward is instead filled with a unique complexity, especially for those like myself serving as commissioned ministers. The complexity is found not in what was said, but in what was left unsaid. While Sutton provides a good distinction between the Office of the Public Ministry and the Priesthood of All Believers, what is left unsaid is the proper place for those called as commissioned ministers. We exist in a sort of in-between state, neither clergy nor laity. My hope is that this book will make the case that commissioned ministers may rightly be defined by more than just what we are not.

There is a tendency to believe that having a high view of the pastoral office means you cannot have a high view of commissioned ministry. Additionally, it is supposed by some that having a high view of commissioned ministry necessitates a lower view of pastoral ministry.[6] My hope is that this book will make the case that this is not an either-or proposition and that one can in fact hold to a high view of pastoral ministry as well as commissioned ministry.

In order to lay out a theology of commissioned ministry, chapter 1 begins by providing descriptions and demographics of those rostered positions that make up commissioned ministry in the LCMS. Chapter 2 examines the distinction between the Priesthood of All Believers and the Office of the Public Ministry. Chapter 3 considers the writings of theologians from Luther to Gerhard as well as the Lutheran Confessions. Chapter 4 examines the development of Lutheran theology on this matter, and specifically the way in which Walther

---

4 Were I called to this congregation, much, though not all, of these would likely be a part of my call.

5 Sutton, *Being Lutheran*, 215–16.

6 An examination of this tendency throughout the history of the LCMS will be explored later on in this book.

formulated his understanding of the Office of the Public Ministry, and the theology of Walther's contemporaries that helped shape his understanding.

Chapter 5 discusses the ways in which the diaconate has been understood in church history. Chapters 6 and 7 lay out the terrain related to the historical development of commissioned ministry in the LCMS. Chapter 6 focuses on the early era of the synod, while chapter 7 focuses on developments in the twentieth century. Chapter 8 examines the biblical case for the place of commissioned ministry in relation to the Office of the Public Ministry. Chapter 9 wraps up the book laying out the final case for a theology of commissioned ministry and a way forward in ministry together, both commissioned and ordained.

My prayer for this book is that it will provide a clear theology of commissioned ministry so current and future church workers, as well as the laity, will better understand the divine call as it relates to our commissioned ministers.

CHAPTER 1

Who Are Commissioned Ministers?

Introduction

As of January 2019, The Lutheran Church—Missouri Synod (LCMS) is served by some 12,936 active rostered church workers.[1] Of these, 6,056 are ordained pastors, and 6,880 are commissioned ministers. There are additionally 401 pastors and 1,837 commissioned ministers on candidate status.[2] Finally, there are 6,669 emeritus workers, 3,206 pastors, and 3,463 commissioned ministers. Additionally, there are many more workers who serve the synod, especially as teachers and church musicians, who are not on the synodical roster.

Behind these numbers are faithful men and women who serve the churches, schools, and recognized service organizations (RSOs) of the LCMS. These commissioned ministers serve in a variety of roles with their own particular emphases. Understanding what each of these commissioned ministers are trained to do will lay a foundation for understanding what commissioned ministry is in the LCMS today.

LUTHERAN TEACHER

There have been Lutheran teachers in the LCMS as long as there has been an LCMS. Building upon the educational traditions of their homeland in Germany, the Saxon immigrants who founded the LCMS often opened a school even before they formally planted a church in a new community. Lutheran schools, during the early years of the synod, had an emphasis on the training up of Lutheran students and for the maintaining of both Lutheran and German heritage.

Though the first teachers in the LCMS where all male, the synod currently rosters both men and women to teach in their early childhood centers, elementary schools, junior high schools, high schools, and colleges/universities. In order to prepare to be called as a Lutheran teacher, future educators typically attend one of the nine colleges and universities that make up the Concordia University System.[3] Not only are Lutheran teachers prepared to learn the craft

---

1 This does not include the many teachers who serve our Lutheran churches who are not on the synodical roster for various reasons.

2 On roster but not currently called to a congregation or other synodical calling body.

3 See www.cus.edu/.

of teaching along with their specialized subject area for high school teachers, but they are also prepared theologically and spiritually in order to work with the pastor(s) and other staff of the congregation as well as the parents of their students.

The Lutheran school and the Lutheran teacher place an emphasis on the formation of the whole student. Specifically, the Lutheran teacher seeks to support the work of the church and the home in the faith formation of their students. The Lutheran teacher is trained to not only teach—math, science, reading, and other subjects—but to do so through the lens of their Christian faith. The Bible is taught and the Christian faith confessed in every course and lesson.

LCMS School Ministry notes that "they study God's Word, share their personal faith story, apply Law and Gospel appropriately, exhibit a passion for ministry, act courageously, equip God's people for service, care for others, demonstrate integrity, and pray."[4] This means that the Lutheran teacher is to be a student of God's Word in addition to the academic subjects that they teach. The Lutheran teacher is able to use Law and Gospel to help students understand not only the way in which God interacts with us as sinners through His Law, but also how in Christ we have been redeemed.

Lutheran teachers do not clock out at 3:00 p.m. when the school day ends or when their grading is complete. They are active members of their congregations. They take an interest in their students and the families of their students, supporting the church in the care of the families of the congregation. Like their public school counterparts, Lutheran school teachers continue to shape and teach students trough extracurricular activities like sports, drama, and music, providing life lessons along with helping further develop valuable skills and talents in their students. However, unlike public school teachers, the Lutheran teacher is expected to conduct all this service with a particular focus in mind.

From the beginning of the day to the end, Lutheran education is all about the Gospel, and the Lutheran teacher is called to bring that Gospel to the children of the congregation and community through the ministry of the Lutheran school. While it is the vocation of all Christian teachers to represent Christ in their teaching, Lutheran teachers are placed in their calls for the expressed purpose of not only teaching the many subjects that are taught in both public and private schools, but also bringing the Gospel into all aspects of that teaching.

Teachers at local Lutheran schools who are not already on the synodical roster can go through a process called "colloquy" to gain the appropriate theo-

---

4 See www.lcms.org/schoolministry.

logical training for certification.[5] Courses are available through CUEnet.[6] Colloquy interviews for admission to the roster of the synod are conducted by their local Concordia University. As of January 2019, there are 5,761 rostered teachers in active service in the LCMS, plus those dual-rostered as teachers and another roster designation (such as DCE or DCO). The current distribution of teachers actively serving in the thirty-five districts of the LCMS can be found below.

FIGURE 1

DISTRICT	**TEACHERS**	New England	8
Atlantic	46	New Jersey	2
California/Nevada/Hawaii	140	North Dakota	10
Central Illinois	160	North Wisconsin	150
Eastern	32	Northern Illinois	471
English	45	Northwest	139
Florida-Georgia	136	Ohio	103
Indiana	426	Oklahoma	33
Iowa East	67	Pacific Southwest	540
Iowa West	32	Rocky Mountain	163
Kansas	66	SELC	18
Michigan	471	South Dakota	27
Mid-South	38	South Wisconsin	602
Minnesota North	27	Southeastern	94
Minnesota South	249	Southern	28
Missouri	492	Southern Illinois	139
Montana	16	Texas	513
Nebraska	273	Wyoming	8
Total Active Teachers:			**5,761**

(Data received: LCMS Rosters and Statistics, January 10, 2019) Candidate and Emeritus data found in Appendix.

5 Colloquy is defined by CUEnet: *The word is Latin for "interview" and is not restricted to use in the church, but frequently appears in a secular context. The Lutheran Church utilizes the colloquy (formal interview) to certify those who seek to be pastors or teachers in Lutheran congregations, but who have not, for one reason or another, had formal training in a college, university, or seminary of the denomination. Usually an abbreviated course of study precedes the interview and is intended to prepare the individual to perform favorably during the interview process.*

6 See http://www.cuenet.edu/.

FIGURE 2

DISTRICT	TEACHERS/DCES	TEACHERS/DCES/DCOS	TEACHERS/DPMS
California/Nevada/Hawaii	2		
Central Illinois	4		
Eastern	4		
English	1		
Florida-Georgia	3		
Indiana	7		1
Iowa East	1		
Iowa West	1		
Kansas	5		
Michigan	17	1	
Mid-South	2		
Minnesota North	1		
Minnesota South	7		
Missouri	8		
Nebraska	9		
North Wisconsin	3		1
Northern Illinois	6		
Northwest	4		1
Ohio	2		
Oklahoma	2		1
Pacific Southwest	10		
Rocky Mountain	6		
South Wisconsin	5	1	
Southeastern	2		
Southern	2		
Southern Illinois	2		
Texas	6		
Totals:	**120**	**2**	**4**

(Data received: LCMS Rosters and Statistics, January 10, 2019) Candidate and Emeritus data found in Appendix.

DEACONESS

The word *deaconess* means "servant." According to Naumann, the Lutheran deaconess is "a trained woman worker called by the proper authorities to do missionary, educational, or charity work within our Lutheran Church."[7] The role of the deaconess has been known in the LCMS since the beginning, though

7 Naumann, *In the Footsteps of Phoebe*, 59.

not utilized until later in its history. The first deaconesses began to serve in the LCMS in 1922. Initially, deaconess training was not provided by either the colleges or seminaries of the LCMS. Concordia University Chicago (then River Forest) began an undergraduate program as the first LCMS training program in 1980. The seminary graduate level programs began in 2002 (Concordia Seminary, St. Louis) and 2003 (Concordia Theological Seminary, Fort Wayne).

Deaconess ministry is a ministry of care. Deaconesses spend their time in both spiritual care as well as social service. Early LCMS deaconess work involved work in orphanages, deaf ministry, and care of the elderly.[8]

While many deaconesses serve through calls to local congregations, many others serve in hospitals, in social service agencies, and as missionaries. Often the Lutheran deaconess is a support to the pastor in providing care to female members of the congregation and community. Whether coming alongside the pastor as he visits women in need of spiritual or pastoral care, or providing this care and support on their own, the Lutheran deaconess is trained to understand the impact of pain, illness, and loss, and is prepared to bring the Gospel of Jesus Christ into those times of struggle. Many deaconesses provide end-of-life care to an increasingly graying population.

Like all commissioned ministers, the Lutheran deaconess is theologically trained. For those receiving their training at one of the seminaries, the person preparing for a calling as a deaconess is able to interact with and learn alongside men preparing for pastoral ministry.

Discussing the deaconess, Löhe,[9] in *About Charity,* notes that "Since there are no longer any congregations like those in the early times, there can be no parish deaconesses like those at that time. . . . Each period of time is destined to undergo changes, and so the deaconess of the nineteenth century must happily adapt herself to change."[10] Thus, the Lutheran deaconess may find herself serving in a variety of care-related ministries.

There are 170 deaconesses actively serving in the LCMS across thirty-one of the thirty-five districts of the synod.

---

8 Olson, *One Ministry Many Roles,* 301.

9 Johann Konrad Wilhelm Löhe (1808–72) was a Bavarian Lutheran pastor who supported both the use of deaconesses as well as the founding of the LCMS, sending confessional pastors to serve.

10 Naumann, *In the Footsteps of Phoebe,* 14.

FIGURE 3

DISTRICT	DCS		
Atlantic	3	Nebraska	6
California/Nevada/Hawaii	5	New England	4
Eastern	3	North Dakota	3
English	5	North Wisconsin	2
Florida-Georgia	11	Northern Illinois	20
Indiana	17	Northwest	8
Iowa East	2	Ohio	4
Iowa West	2	Oklahoma	3
Kansas	1	Pacific Southwest	6
Michigan	8	Rocky Mountain	22
Mid-South	1	SELC	1
Minnesota North	2	South Wisconsin	10
Minnesota South	4	Southeastern	6
Missouri	28	Southern	2
Montana	1	Southern Illinois	2
		Texas	10
Total Deaconesses:			**170**

(Data received: LCMS Rosters and Statistics, January 10, 2019) Candidate and Emeritus data found in Appendix.

DIRECTOR OF CHRISTIAN EDUCATION

Growing out of Lutheran teaching, the Director of Christian Education (DCE) has a history in the LCMS going back to 1959. Though having a much briefer history than the Lutheran teacher or deaconess, the DCE has been providing leadership in many congregations in the area of Christian education and its related fields since its inception.

> A Director of Christian Education (DCE) is a lifespan educational leader prepared for team ministry in a congregational setting and is certified, called, and commissioned by The Lutheran Church—Missouri Synod (LCMS). A DCE, empowered by the Holy Spirit, plans, administers, and assesses ministry that nurtures and equips people in the Body of Christ for spiritual maturity, service and witnessing in their homes, jobs, congregations, communities, and the world.[11]

Though sometimes perceived as a calling for the young, DCEs of all ages and stages in their careers serve congregations, schools, and recognized service organizations (RSOs) throughout the LCMS. Whether providing instruction

11 "Director of Christian Education (DCE) Program." *Concordia University Irvine,* www.cui.edu/dce.

directly or equipping volunteers[12] to join in the educational ministries of the congregation, DCEs are involved with all ages. Many are called specifically to serve in children's, youth, or adult ministry. Many others are generalists called to provide leadership across multiple age ranges and in a variety of settings.

The ministry of the DCE may be seen through his or her leadership in Sunday School, Vacation Bible School, mission trips, youth gatherings, retreats, youth groups, parenting seminars, confirmation, and many other educational ministries. To prepare for such a broad role, DCEs are trained in theology as well as educational theory.

Further, a DCE also fulfills the following roles:

> Ministry Leader: Heart for full-time service in the church
>
> Christian Educator: Strong theological base to teach the Bible
>
> Care Minister: Dynamic character, willing to listen to and care for the needs of others
>
> Life-Span Minister: Compassion for people of all ages and backgrounds.[13]

The ministry of the DCE is a support to the pastor that may take many different shapes depending on the needs of the local church as well as the life stage and skill/experience of the individual DCE. While the younger DCE may find his or her nights alive with a noise of lock-ins and retreats, the more seasoned DCE may be called upon to provide holistic ministry to the family. What unites the ministry of the DCE across these various life stages and ministry emphases is a passion for teaching the faith through well-formed theological reflection to members of the congregation and community across the life span in developmentally appropriate and creative ways. There are five DCE programs in the Concordia University System. They all offer traditional undergraduate certification. Concordia University Irvine offers graduate-level certification via distance learning for adult learners seeking a career change later in life and for those already in DCE-related ministry in a local congregation.

There are 591 DCEs currently in active ministry across the synod in thirty-three of thirty-five districts plus 129 dual-rostered (see figure 2).

---

12 As will be discussed later when dealing with the Priesthood of All Believers, all members of the Body of Christ are called to serve in some capacity. There is a distinction between the voluntary nature of some service and the public nature of being called by a gathering of the Body of Christ (congregation, school, district, synod, or RSO) into a specific form of ministry service.

13 "Director of Christian Education (DCE) Program." *Concordia University Irvine,* www.cui.edu/dce.

FIGURE 4

DISTRICT	DCES	New England	1
Atlantic	2	New Jersey	1
California/Nevada/Hawaii	22	North Dakota	4
Central Illinois	14	North Wisconsin	19
Eastern	4	Northern Illinois	25
English	5	Northwest	29
Florida-Georgia	21	Ohio	11
Indiana	27	Oklahoma	7
Iowa East	6	Pacific Southwest	62
Iowa West	10	Rocky Mountain	19
Kansas	17	SELC	3
Michigan	26	South Dakota	6
Mid-South	7	South Wisconsin	10
Minnesota North	9	Southeastern	25
Minnesota South	40	Southern	6
Missouri	36	Southern Illinois	4
Nebraska	23	Texas	91
Total DCEs:			**591**

(Data received: LCMS Rosters and Statistics, January 10, 2019) Candidate and Emeritus data found in Appendix.

DIRECTOR OF CHRISTIAN OUTREACH

Like the deaconess and the DCE, the Director of Christian Outreach (DCO) was established by the LCMS to support the work of the pastor. While the DCE is focused on Christian education, the DCO is focused on outreach. Just as the DCE is an equipper focused on Christian education, the DCO equips and supports the members of the congregation in their outreach and presentation of the Gospel to the community around them. The DCO is formed theologically with a missiological[14] emphasis.

The ministerial formation of DCOs takes place alongside DCEs at Concordia University, St. Paul. This provides a connection to life-span ministry that impacts how the DCO is able to equip the local church to reach out to it community with the Gospel. The DCO may be seen as a missional type of role, whose ministry may include establishing a church plant for a new congregation or attempting to revitalize a more established church.

The ministry of the DCO is naturally focused more on those outside the church than those within its walls. Yet, while the DCO keeps the needs of those

14 In this context, what is meant by *missiological* is an emphasis in the practice of ministry on the intersection of the Christian faith with the larger culture for the purpose of outreach, apologetics, and evangelism.

who have yet to hear the Gospel or who have not yet come to saving faith in Christ in the forefront of his or her mind, the DCO balances that ministry with the work of equipping the members of the location congregation to engage in outreach as well. The ministry of the DCO has been established in order to better equip the local congregation to understand the context in which God has placed their ministry and to formulate and execute a Spirit-led strategy to reach that community with the Gospel.

There are currently seventeen active DCOs serving in eleven districts, plus four who are dual certified (see figure 2).

FIGURE 5

DISTRICT	**DCOS**	Nebraska	1
Iowa West	1	North Wisconsin	1
Michigan	2	Northern Illinois	2
Minnesota North	1	Rocky Mountain	1
Minnesota South	4	Southeastern	1
Missouri	1	Texas	2
Total DCOs:			**17**

(Data received: LCMS Rosters and Statistics, January 10, 2019) Candidate and Emeritus data found in Appendix.

DIRECTOR OF PARISH MUSIC

The relatively recent development of the Director of Parish Music (DPM) has elevated the role of the church musician within the LCMS and their support of the ministry of the pastor in worship. While Lutheranism has had a more than solid history in music (think of Luther the hymnwriter here as well as Bach, who was called to serve at St. Nicholas and St. Thomas in Leipzig), the DPM places that tradition more formally within the ministry of the local congregation.

In addition to a strong theological training, DPMs are as broadly trained musically as possible due to the variety of ministry needs and musical styles found in the local church. Training may range from proficiency on the organ to handbells, choir, and/or the direction of a praise band for contemporary forms of worship arts.

> A Director of Parish Music (DPM) is a gifted music leader prepared for team ministry in a parish church setting and is certified, called, and commissioned by The Lutheran Church—Missouri Synod (LCMS). A DPM may function as a Minister of Music, an Organist or Lead Guitarist, Choral/Instrumental Conductor, Music Teacher, Worship Arts Director, Leader of Contemporary Worship, or quite often a combination of two or more of the above list.[15]

15 "Director of Parish Music (DPM) Program." *Concordia University Irvine*, www.cui.edu/dpm.

DPM positions may be full time in larger congregations. They may involve additional responsibilities with an affiliated Lutheran school. They may also include children's, youth, or family ministry, or may be bi-vocational with another role outside the ministry of the local church. Training to become a DPM is available at seven of the Concordia universities. There are seventy-four DPMs currently active in the LCMS across twenty-two districts.

FIGURE 6

DISTRICT	DPMS		
Atlantic	1	Nebraska	3
Central Illinois	1	North Wisconsin	3
English	3	Northern Illinois	4
Florida-Georgia	1	Northwest	1
Indiana	4	Pacific Southwest	7
Kansas	1	Rocky Mountain	4
Michigan	8	South Wisconsin	6
Mid-South	4	Southeastern	2
Minnesota South	4	Southern	1
Missouri	8	Southern Illinois	1
Montana	1	Texas	6
Total DPMs:			**74**

(Data received: LCMS Rosters and Statistics, January 10, 2019) Candidate and Emeritus data found in Appendix.

DIRECTOR OF FAMILY LIFE MINISTRY

The newest rostered position in the LCMS is the Director of Family Life Ministry (DFLM), having been approved in convention in 2004. The DFLM is "called to equip, support and build strong Christian marriages and families that live well through each life span as well as church programming for children and youth ministry to pass on faith in Jesus Christ to future generations."[16] In addition to certification in the LCMS, DFLMs are also certified Family Life Educators by the National Council on Family Relations. This dual certification is reflected in the combination of theological and social science education that DFLMs receive to prepare them to support the ministry of the pastor as he ministers to the families of his congregation and community.

DFLMs serve the church by developing life-stage programs to build and equip strong, healthy families through programming, family life education, and mentoring. They are prepared to provide training for parents in shaping faith at home and in church, premarriage education and marriage enrichment training, parent education classes throughout the life span, human sexuality training,

16 Ben Freudenburg, email message to author, January 4, 2017.

training for families with members in the later years, and non-nuclear family training. The DFLM seeks to serve the church by supporting the family holistically. Viewing the family as a system, the DFLM is able to support the family through the various changes confronted throughout the stages of the life cycle. Though often doing similar work that a DCE might, the DFLM is prepared with a deeper base of social science training specifically aimed at preparing them for this ministry with the family, rather than the educational emphasis of the DCE.

The synod's only training program for DFLMs is housed at Concordia University Ann Arbor and connected to the ministry of the Concordia Center for the Family. There are forty-two DFLMs active in the LCMS currently across fourteen districts.

FIGURE 7

DISTRICT	**DFLMS**	Nebraska	2
English	1	Northern Illinois	2
Florida-Georgia	2	Northwest	2
Indiana	1	Ohio	4
Michigan	23	Rocky Mountain	1
Mid-South	1	Southeastern	1
Minnesota South	1	Texas	1
Missouri	1		
Total DFLMs:			**42**

(Data received: LCMS Rosters and Statistics, January 10, 2019) Candidate and Emeritus data found in Appendix.

LAY MINISTER

The Lay Minister is the final commissioned minister to be examined. This ministry varies depending on the talents of the individual, the training track taken in preparation, and the needs of the local congregation. A Lay Minister may be involved in evangelism, visitation, Christian education, youth ministry, senior ministry, church administration, member assimilation, and spiritual gifts administration, among other areas of local congregational ministry. Lay Ministers are trained in theology as well as their area of specialization. The synod's only training program for Lay Ministers is housed at Concordia University Wisconsin, where they have been training Lay Ministers for over fifty years.[17]

The Lay Ministry training program also includes an online component specifically designed for older, working adults. This program fits particularly well with individuals who are already working in a church but who do not have a credential that would allow them to be called and placed on the roster of the LCMS. There are seventy-nine Lay Ministers serving in twenty districts.

17 Concordia University Wisconsin offers training to be a Lay Minister through their Director of Church Ministries Program.

FIGURE 8

DISTRICT	LAY MINS.	Montana	1
Atlantic	1	Nebraska	3
California/Nevada/Hawaii	1	New England	2
Central Illinois	2	North Wisconsin	11
English	3	Northern Illinois	16
Indiana	2	Oklahoma	5
Iowa West	1	Pacific Southwest	2
Michigan	1	South Wisconsin	5
Minnesota North	2	Southeastern	9
Minnesota South	2	Texas	4
Missouri	7		
Total Lay Ministers:			**79**

(Data received: LCMS Rosters and Statistics, March 2018) Candidate and Emeritus data found in Appendix.

CONCLUSION[18]

It is rather easy to see the diversity of service provided by commissioned ministers. While there is overlap and parallel work done by individuals from different roster classifications, this diversity of training and emphasis in ministry enriches congregations across the LCMS. In addition to the active commissioned ministers noted above, there are some 1,837 candidates who remain on roster while seeking calls or taking intentional time off between calls. Further, there are 3,463 emeritus commissioned ministers who have retired.

Each of these offices was established to support the ministry of the pastor. Individuals in each are theologically trained and have specialized training and skills, which pastors typically do not, for specific aspects of a congregation's ministry. The training of commissioned ministers is substantively different than that of pastors. Whereas pastors in the LCMS get a deeper and broader theological education than commissioned ministers, their seminary education only includes one course in teaching and one course in pastoral care/counseling. The specialized training of commissioned ministers is specifically designed to provide workers who can support the pastor in those areas of education and care. These are areas of ministry that the synod has determined are important and deserving of specialized attention. Thus, the synod has created these offices, authorized training programs across the Concordia University System, and encourages local congregations to call commissioned ministers to serve alongside their pastors.

18 Parish Assistants are not included here due to their small numbers, only nine serving in active ministry as of March 2018.

CHAPTER 2

The Priesthood of All Believers & the Office of the Public Ministry

WHAT IS A PRIEST?

One of the rediscoveries of the Reformation was the Priesthood of All Believers. Rather than having to rely solely upon a priest to intercede on one's behalf with God, the reformers taught that each individual Christian was able to approach God in prayer in the name of Jesus Christ. In order for this doctrine of the church to make sense as it relates to the focus of this book, it must be understood in its proper context as it relates to the Office of the Public Ministry. To begin unpacking this theological concept, it would be helpful to understand what a priest is in the first place.

When traversing the desert at Sinai, Moses and Aaron were called to perform mediatorial duties on behalf of the people of Israel. Moses did this as he ascended the mountain in order to seek the presence of God and receive His Word in both the form of the Law (Ten Commandments) as well as the Gospel in rudimentary proclamation—the promise of the conquest of Canaan (Exodus 23:20ff.). In Exodus 19:11, we learn that God instructed Moses to "put limits for the people around the mountain." The people were to avoid coming close even to the mountain lest they be put to death by the holy God. Moses, sinner though he was, was called upon by God to prophetically bring God's Law to the people.

Aaron was set aside as the first high priest of the recently baptized people of Israel (Exodus 14:22; 40:12; 1 Corinthians 10:2). He was called upon to offer sacrifices on behalf of the people to atone for their sins. These sacrifices provided a covering for the sins of Aaron and Moses as well.

The tribe of Levi was selected to be the tribe from which the priests for the people of Israel were to be drawn (Numbers 3). As a tribe, they were to be both separated from yet integrated into the larger nation. They were not to receive a land of their own like the other tribes, but were to spread throughout the whole of the nation. Their task was to present offerings on behalf of the people as God required them in order to atone for the sins of the nation.

One of the key aspects of their role as priests was their obedience to the instructions of God. The priests were to approach God only as God demanded, not as they deemed it appropriate of their own volition. He prescribed the rituals intended for purification for the priests as they went about their work. The sacrificial offerings of the people were to be presented in accord with the instructions outlined by the Lord.

Priests were needed to provide mediatorial service to atone for the disobedience of the people; this included atoning for their own disobedience as well. God provided the details of how the sacrifices were to be properly presented to Him. These steps needed to be followed in exacting detail. Through this offering by the Levitical priests, God provided the divine means by which His sinful and fallen people would be able to come before Him, be washed clean, and be restored to a right relationship with the Lord.

In Leviticus, we learn about the fate of Nadab and Abihu, the sons of Aaron. Luther explains the fate of the sons of Aaron this way in his explanation of the misuse of the Mass.

> Let us further consider these noble high priests—who now shamelessly dare to call themselves princes, namely the bishops—so that we may see and recognize the whole body of the devil with all its members. Here again I should like to renew my premise, which ought to be maintained intact by every Christian, that everything which occurs outside the Scriptures, especially in matters pertaining to God, comes from the devil. God showed this in Nadab and Abihu [Lev. 10:1–3], when he did not wish the strange fire to be offered, and in this way vehemently condemned the conduct of divine matters otherwise than he himself has commanded. "I will show myself holy," he says, "among those who are near me" [Lev. 10:3]. How much more will he condemn and grow angry if one not only makes some new thing without scriptural authority, but also extinguishes his command and institution, as when unbelieving Ahaz made the brazen altar into a sundial and set the altar of Damascus in God's temple.[1]

What was the nature of this unauthorized fire? We do not specifically learn this from the text. Rather the emphasis of this section of Scripture is on the unauthorized nature of the fire. This was an offering of worship according to the will of Nadab and Abihu, not according to the will of the Lord.

The priests were therefore to follow the instructions and guidance of the Lord in how they conducted the ministry on His behalf to His people. Norman Nagel notes that a priest is always to be seen in relation to someone else.[2] One cannot be a priest for himself or on his own behalf. God places one in a priestly role on behalf of another as noted in 1 Peter 2:9: "But you are a chosen race, a

---

1 LW 36:154.

2 Nagel, "Luther and the Priesthood of All Believers," 278.

royal priesthood, a holy nation." A priest is chosen by God to mediate His grace to His people and to the rest of the nations.

The Lord took great time in walking through exactly what He expected of the priests. He prescribed what they were to wear when they offered sacrifices on behalf of the people and the specific manner in which they were to offer those sacrifices. Neither the priests themselves nor the people they served were holy. They could not by self-chosen sacrifices or ceremonies either approach God or establish fellowship with Him, the kind of fellowship He had with Adam and Eve in the garden. God established the priestly office, setting apart men to represent the people before God. These priests, being sinners as the rest of the people, followed the instructions of the Lord for their own purification prior to serving the people as His priests; prior to purification, they were not more or less holy than the rest of Israel, and their own unholiness prevented an approach to God.

THE ROMAN PRIEST

The priest in the Roman Catholic Church of Luther's day, to a certain extent, functioned in a similar manner as the ancient priests of Israel. The people were expected to have their worship of God mediated by the priests or saints. One simply did not conceive of approaching the Holy God on their own. If the individual believer needed absolution from the "holier" priest, much better it would be then for that same holier priest to pray for the individual.

When the printing press began to make the Bible more readily available, Rome objected. The role of the priest was to present the interpretation of Scripture as determined by the church. For the priest was not only necessary in order for the common Christian to pray to God, but also for the common Christian to receive the Word back from God. The priest was the communication conduit by which man spoke to God and God to man.

The average person was unable to approach even the Word of God, let alone God Himself on his own behalf. As Moses had instructed that limits surrounded Sinai, the Roman Catholic Church in the sixteenth century supposed that it, too, was keeping the people of God at a safe distance from the Lord's holiness.

While this distance was intended to protect the people from the potential of the misinterpretation of Scripture—something Rome accused the Reformation of unleashing and perhaps with some justification—the result was fraught with its own unintended consequences. Further, while some might take for granted the easy availability of the Bible, access to God's Word was limited not only by the dictates of the church, but also by the immense cost of producing a Bible. With the invention of the printing press and the emphasis on Scripture on the part of the reformers, the Scriptures became far more available and in the vernacular of the people in many countries.

An elaborate hierarchy, consisting of priests, bishops, archbishops, cardinals, and the pontiff himself, had developed over the centuries. Though the Roman Catholic Church had enabled that hierarchical structure in order to guard the truth of God, it lacked a procedure to identify and counter unbiblical teaching on the part of church officials, and thus corruption had been able to creep into the church. In the fifteenth century, a prior attempt at reform by John Huss failed in part due to the ability of the church to stamp out teachings counter to their own. Unlike Huss, Luther enjoyed the protection of his elector due to the complicated political system among the German states during the sixteenth century. Further, with the invention of the printing press Luther had greater access to bring his ideas to the people. The spread and defense of teaching, whether the truth of the Scriptures or even heresy, in those days involved political and technological means even as it was a religious pursuit.

Thus, the local priest was not expected nor often trained to critically examine the Bible in order to provide the most accurate teaching of God's Word to the people. Rather, the people were to receive from the priest the teachings of the Roman Catholic Church as determined and prescribed further up the church hierarchy, by the intellectual and ecclesiastical betters of their local priest.

The priest was also present to hear the confession of the parishioner and determine the penance required for forgiveness by God, prior to participation in the Mass. The faithful Christian believer was kept at a distance from God, just as the ancient Israelites had been in the desert of Sinai—though for a different purpose. The practice of prayer to saints developed in the church, creating an alternative to prayer directly to the Father, in the name of Christ the Son, by the power of the Holy Spirit. Rather than coming to God directly for their forgiveness, many turned to their priest and/or prayed to Mary and the saints to speak on their behalf to God.

This is not to assert an entirely negative view of confession to one's pastor, something Luther maintained as he sought to remove the mandate for private confession and the enumeration of sins. Both private and corporate confession are good, right, and proper and ought to be encouraged. The distinction at this point is rather the way in which the forgiveness of sins was not merely announced by a pastor in the name of Christ, but rather that the Roman priest was understood to mediate God's grace.

Rather than merely announcing the grace of God in His forgiveness of our sins, the Roman priest claims participation in the mediatorial work of Christ. A subordinate role to that of Christ, but a role nonetheless. The assertion of this role can be seen in the requirement that all Catholics go to confession at least annually, the requirement for penance in order to receive forgiveness, as well as the claim that forgiveness was only truly available through the mediation of the priest.

It is further worth keeping in mind that the Roman Catholic sacramental understanding of ordination is at odds with the Lutheran understanding, in that the Roman Catholic priest was believed to be endowed through ordination with an "indelible" character that enabled him to do the Mass. Thus it is through this "indelible" character that the sacrament of penance is performed. Only the priest is able to perform such a sacramental act.

Luther's concern was not to eliminate the Roman priest. Rather, Nagel points out that Luther sought to ensure that the popery of the Roman priesthood would not encroach upon the priestly work of Christ.[3]

PRIESTHOOD OF ALL BELIEVERS

Some might argue that the Priesthood of All Believers is one of the most neglected or most misunderstood/misused of Luther's Reformation teachings.[4] Discussing what Peter means by Holy Priesthood in 1 Peter 2:5, Luther states:

> We have argued extensively that those who are called priests today are not priests in the sight of God. And we have substantiated this with what Peter says here. Therefore understand it well, and if someone comes along and wants to explain it—as some have done—by saying that Peter is speaking about a twofold priesthood, namely, about external and spiritual priests, then ask him to put spectacles on to be able to see and take hellebore to sweep out his brain.[5]

In this way, Luther explains that the Roman Catholic concept of the priest was in fact antithetical with a biblical notion of priesthood. It is evident from the passage that those whom Peter is calling priest are not merely a special class of believer such as the Roman priest, but are in fact all believers. The recent CTCR document *The Royal Priesthood* affirms this, noting that the priestly calling is to all believers.[6]

Responding to the reformers, the Council of Trent affirmed the Catholic teaching of the conjoined nature of the priesthood and Holy Communion. The priest was necessary to receive the grace of God poured out in the death of Christ.[7] Luther however, makes a distinction between the priesthood of Leviticus, which the priesthood of Roman Catholicism is modeled upon, and that of Christ in his discussion of Psalm 110:

---

3 Nagel, "Luther and the Priesthood of All Believers," 281.

4 The publication of the CTCR document *The Royal Priesthood: Identity and Mission* in late 2018 sought to address this neglect.

5 LW 30:52–53.

6 The Lutheran Church—Missouri Synod, *The Royal Priesthood: Identity and Mission*, 14.

7 James Waterworth, *The Council of Trent The Canons and Decrees of the Sacred and Ecumenical Council of Trent*, 170–71.

> Hereby he makes a clear distinction between Christ's priestly office and the Levitical priesthood. Thus he crashes and breaks through all of Moses; he acts as though he knew nothing of him. Indeed, he intentionally adds the qualification "after the order of Melchizedek" that no one might imagine that Christ is a priest like Aaron, or mistake His priestly office for the equivalent of what is commanded and ordained in the Law.[8]

Thus, in Christ, we have the only true priest that we need. Melchizedek stands as a unique figure in Scripture. His story is brief and unusual. He seems to come from nowhere and just as quickly return to nowhere. Yet, this is the context that Christ is placed in, by the psalmist as well as the author of Hebrews.

With Christ as our priest, we need not seek another priest through whom we are to approach God the Father to seek His forgiveness, guidance, and wisdom. We can seek the will of God from the source. As royal priests, our mediatorial work involves our prayer. Prayer for ourselves, as well as prayer for others.[9] Luther emphasized both the direct access of the Scriptures by the non-ordained as well as the direct ability of the believer to pray to the Father, in the name of Christ the Son, through the guidance of the Holy Spirit.

Further, according to 1 Peter all Christians are in fact priests, in that they are able to speak words of forgiveness to one another in the name of Christ. It is not the role of the clergy alone to present the Word of God to those in need of a Savior. The pastor speaks on behalf of Christ publicly[10] to the entire congregation and even in private pastoral care because of his call, but he is not the only one who can use the Word to tell others about Christ. All Christians are enabled by the Holy Spirit to bring the Word to one another and to those outside the church who need to hear the Gospel. All Christians are able to speak words of comfort and consolation to one another. All Christians are able to speak the truth in love, offering correction from the Law as needed. All Christians are able to remind one another of the forgiveness, freely given in Christ to each of us. God's grace is spoken by pastors as well as by fellow believers. Gathered together, Christians study God's Word and assist one another in the interpretation of the Scriptures. While there is indeed a need for the trained guidance of pastors in this task, through the ministry of the Holy Spirit, Christians are not left ill equipped and unable to read and learn for themselves.

With his classic directness, Luther stresses that:

---

8 LW 13:309.

9 *The Royal Priesthood: Identity and Mission*, 16.

10 Though much more will be said later in the book, it may help to clarify here that when the term *public* is used in this context it is not denoting something done where others can see the act taking place. Rather, it refers to the individual having been placed or called to that form of service by some gathering of the Body of Christ (congregation, school, district, synod, or RSO).

> Indeed, all Christians are priests, and all priests are Christians. Worthy of anathema is any assertion that a priest is anything else than a Christian. For such an assertion has no support in the Word of God and is based only on human opinions, on ancient usage, or on the opinions of the majority, any one of which is ineffectual to establish an article of faith without sacrilege and offense, as I have sufficiently shown elsewhere.[11]

Luther had little patience for the Roman conception of the priesthood as a holy order separate from the average Christian. For Luther, it was critically important for all believers to recognize their role as priests and not place the Roman priest in a mediating role between God and man. This would only bring humanity back to a state prior to the cross of Christ and return us to our need for a Savior. We have that Savior, and it is in His name, in the name of Christ Jesus our Lord, that we can boldly approach the throne of the Father, seeking His grace and favor in prayer and humble confession.

THE OFFICE OF THE PUBLIC MINISTRY

With an empowered Priesthood of All Believers, is there a necessity for pastors and other church workers?

> Living for God is not about fleeing the work to which God has called you so that you can live in a monastery praying all day; rather, living for God is about faithfully being used by God to perform the work to which He has called you. To be certain, the Priesthood of All Believers does not negate the need for pastors. . . . The Office of the Ministry is established by Christ and conferred upon the individual pastor through the call of the congregation. Does this negate the Priesthood of All Believers? By no means! . . . The difference is in vocation. God has called different people to different vocations.[12]

God calls every Christian to be a member of the Priesthood of All Believers, but he calls only some to carry out the Office of the Public Ministry. Thus, the Office of Public Ministry can be defined as those called by the Priesthood of All Believers to serve in ministry on their behalf. All those baptized into Christ may rightly be called priests, but this does not imply that all the baptized are called to the Office of the Public Ministry.[13]

Luther states that "one is born to be priest, one becomes a minister."[14] A pastor is not born a pastor. He is not baptized a pastor. Rather, having been trained by the church or church body, he is called by God through the local

---

11 LW 40:19.

12 Sutton, *Being Lutheran,* 215–16.

13 Nagel, "Luther and the Priesthood of All Believers," 285.

14 LW 40:18.

congregation and placed by God through the means of this call as a pastor in the Office of the Public Ministry. It would not do for individuals to declare themselves to be pastors and assume a role that the church does not entrust them with. Think of the chaos that would ensue if this Sunday, as an elder of my church, I thought that I could handle the sermon better than our pastor and simply attempted to take over. The pastoral office exists by God's command. It is due to that command that the church both locally and within a larger church body determines who is able to serve in that office and affirms the scriptural qualifications for said office. Thus, not only would chaos ensue if I were to preach without a call, but I would violate the express command of God in taking upon myself an office that ought to be conferred by others, not assumed by an individual of their own will and self-perceived authority.

This is, to some extent, what Paul was writing against in 1 Corinthians. The Corinthian Church was having a number of issues related to their practice of worship. Starting in chapter 11, Paul begins by expressing his concerns over the ways in which the Lord's Supper was being handled. It would seem that rather than sharing this sacred meal together with dignity and decorum, members of the Corinthian Church were gorging themselves on the bread and wine, while the body and blood was dishonored. Try to picture members of your congregation consuming so much wine that they were getting drunk. Try to imagine the bread being consumed in large quantity by some, leaving none for others.

It was the practice of the church in Corinth to celebrate a community meal when they partook in the Lord's Supper. Unlike our modern practice, these local house churches at times consisted of people in various rooms around the home. The wealthy, it would seem, were stuffing themselves with the body and blood of Christ and leaving little to none for poorer members of the church in other rooms.

Paul reminds them what this meal is to be about and calls them back to their unity in Christ despite the diversity in their social standing. He reminds the wealthy that they have their own homes for eating and drinking and not to confuse those meals with the Lord's Supper. We share this meal together as the Body of Christ, united, sharing a common bond and purpose.

Paul points out in 1 Corinthians 12 that this Body of Christ is gathered by our Lord as the local congregation and is uniquely gifted. Each member of the Body is endowed with his or her own spiritual gifts. These gifts are from God and are not merely personal skills that we might be otherwise tempted to brag about. Through this variety of gifts, God so equips and calls the church together in order that the church might function well as a unit in mission to a dying and fallen world.

Moving to chapter 13, Paul takes up how this Body of Christ is to live and serve in our life together: We are to love one another. This love is to be well beyond the kind of love that the world settles for. This love is to be selfless as Christ's love for His Church is selfless. Putting others first in love, we learn that

> Love is patient, love is kind. It does not envy, it does not boast, it is not proud. It does not dishonor others, it is not self-seeking, it is not easily angered, it keeps no record of wrongs. Love does not delight in evil but rejoices with the truth. It always protects, always trusts, always hopes, always perseveres. Love never fails. (1 Corinthians 13:4–8)

Finally, in 1 Corinthians 14, Paul turns to the worship life of the church, and building on the prior chapters, he discusses the reality that God calls certain individuals and gifts them in such a way so as to publicly serve the church. Thus not everyone is to assume a public role in the leadership of the congregation.

> What then shall we say, brothers and sisters? When you come together, each of you has a hymn, or a word of instruction, a revelation, a tongue or an interpretation. Everything must be done so that the church may be built up. If anyone speaks in a tongue, two—or at the most three—should speak, one at a time, and someone must interpret. If there is no interpreter, the speaker should keep quiet in the church and speak to himself and to God.
>
> Two or three prophets should speak, and the others should weigh carefully what is said. And if a revelation comes to someone who is sitting down, the first speaker should stop. For you can all prophesy in turn so that everyone may be instructed and encouraged. The spirits of prophets are subject to the control of prophets. For God is not a God of disorder but of peace—as in all the congregations of the Lord's people. (1 Corinthians 14:27–33)

Thus, I am not at liberty to step into the pulpit on Sunday, even if I get the notion that my pastor might not be as good a communicator as I believe myself to be. There is a reason that members of the local church do not appoint themselves to offices that are not entrusted to them.

Koehler discusses the difference between the personal priesthood of all Christians and the public ministry this way:

> As we distinguish between a private citizen and a public official, so must we distinguish between an individual Christian and the called minister of the congregation ... the one acts as an individual Christian on the basis of his royal priesthood, which may not be curtailed in any manner; the other acts on the basis of the call he received from his fellow-Christians. One acts, under God, in his own name; the other acts, under God, in the name of the congregation which has called him.[15]

---

15 Koehler, *A Summary of Christian Doctrine,* 265.

Individual Christians do not decide that they are pastors. God calls them through the church into that office. There is both an internal and an external call. A young man who believes that he is called to be a pastor may have an internal call. However, as he studies his way through seminary and even seeks his first call, if there is no congregation to call him, he lacks an external call. The key is that those called into the public ministry are to be both called and authorized by and on behalf of the royal priesthood.[16]

Each individual Christian is empowered by the Holy Spirit to speak the Word of God into the lives of those placed by God into their own path. But as Koehler rightly distinguishes, this proclamation of the Gospel is a private matter. This is an individual act of the baptized priest, and not done publicly on behalf of the church, universal or local. On the other hand, certain individuals are called into public service by the church and placed in their office in order to proclaim the Gospel publicly on behalf of the church.

Luther puts it this way:

> This is the way to distinguish between the office of preaching, or the ministry, and the general priesthood of all baptized Christians. The preaching office is no more than a public service which happens to be conferred upon someone by the entire congregation, all the members of which are priests.[17]

One further clarification might prove helpful. What of the Bible study teacher or small-group leader who does his or her teaching in a public setting? Is this a public ministry? While this ministry is done in a public setting, that does not make this a public ministry. The distinction under consideration here is rather related to whether the ministry is public (on behalf of the church) or individual. The Bible study teacher is accountable to the church, but is exercising service individually as a part of the Priesthood of All Believers, not as one called to public ministry. For the sake of good teaching and order, a home study, which is conducted by members of a congregation, is not the public teaching of the congregation, though good pastoral care would call the pastor to take an active interest in the study.

Additionally, much of what is done by those entrusted with the Office of the Public Ministry is done privately. For example, the private confession and absolution the pastor provides to individual members of the church throughout the week is just as much a part of his public ministry as the public or corporate confession and absolution we take part in each Sunday. This is not an individual act but rather still his public ministry regardless of the setting in which the ministry is conducted.

---

16 The Lutheran Church—Missouri Synod, *The Royal Priesthood: Identity and Mission*, 15.

17 LW 13:332.

In like manner, hearing the individual (or personal) confession of a member (or person) in his church office is no less a part of the public ministry of the pastor. Rather it is the placement of the pastor into the Office of the Public Ministry that distinguishes his ministry from that of the laity, not the number of people who bear witness to any particular aspect of that ministry.

> The first office, that of the ministry of the Word, therefore, is common to all Christians. This is clear, from what I have already said, and from 1 Pet. 2[:9], "You are a royal priesthood that you may declare the wonderful deeds of him who called you out of darkness into his marvelous light." I ask, who are these who are called out of darkness into marvelous light? Is it only the shorn and anointed masks? Is it not all Christians? And Peter not only gives them the right, but the command, to declare the wonderful deeds of God, which certainly is nothing else than to preach the Word of God. … So, as there is no other proclamation in the ministry of the Word than that which is common to all, that of the wonderful deed of God, so there is no other priesthood than that which is spiritual and universal, as Peter here defines it.[18]

Dean Nadasdy points out that "both pastor and laity have a calling through which God works, even though their offices may differ."[19] Those who serve the church and are called into the Office of the Public Ministry are thus not a special class or more holy order of Christian. Their service is worthy of respect and should be held in high esteem, but they have the same call to spread the Gospel as all Christians. Those in public ministry are held to a higher standard, but this does not negate the private work of the laity.

The Office of the Public Ministry is of divine origin. This office is not the creation of the church. Individuals are placed into this office through the Spirit-led work of the local church, but the office is not of their own making. This is important to keep in mind. It is not merely that there is work to be done in the local church and thus a pastor is hired to take on that work. We may at times hear the calling of a pastor discussed in terms that might lead one to conclude the he is merely being hired, but there is a substantive difference between the calling of a pastor and the hiring of nursery care workers for Sunday morning. The pastor is not the CEO of the congregation. There may be great value in the pastor's leadership or vision-casting abilities, but these are not the substance of his ministry. The church cannot hire a member of the flock, even a very godly and theologically sound man, simply because he speaks well. These surface-level functions do not make the pastor a pastor.

As Lutherans, we make a big deal about vocation. Each of us has multiple vocations in which we serve both God and humanity in His name. While Luther

---

18 LW 40:21–22.

19 Nadasdy, "Vocation and Mission," 51.

was right to assert that vocation is not merely related to taking on holy orders as was the practice in the church of his day, we ought not confuse his point with an attempt to equate the vocation of those in public ministry with those who are not.

WHERE DOES THE COMMISSIONED MINISTER FIT?

The question then is this: Just who is able to be entrusted with the Office of the Public Ministry? Is this office merely to be seen as synonymous with the pastoral office? What are we to do with commissioned ministers like Lutheran teachers, DCEs, and others?

The typical dichotomy of clergy and laity, as is used in discussions on the Office of the Public Ministry and Priesthood of All Believers, fails to address the status of those in auxiliary, or helping, offices. Those who serve as commissioned ministers in the LCMS are bearers of these auxiliary calls. As such, workers are installed and commissioned to their various offices, but the question remains: Are those who serve as commissioned ministers truly public ministers of the Gospel?

The relationship of auxiliary offices to the public ministry is laid out by Eugene Klug:

> It naturally follows from this that other offices constituted within and by the church may, indeed, have a God-pleasing purpose and function, but they would in each case derive in some way from the one divinely ordained office, and thus be auxiliary to or derive from it. They devolve from a felt existential need, and are created in Christian liberty to be of assistance to the pastoral office. So, for example, even the apostles saw the necessity for deacons to assist them in their multiple duties in the growing church, Acts 6:1–15; Philippians 1:1; 1 Timothy 5:17.[20]

Klug further clarifies that the authority of these auxiliary offices ultimately belongs to the pastoral office. It is only in the exercise of the Christian liberty of the local church or larger denominational church body that this authority is extended to and placed in an auxiliary office (p. 269). The changing ministry needs of the local church gives rise to new auxiliary offices.

In a 2018 presentation, Rev. Dr. Joel Lehenbauer of the LCMS Commission on Theology and Church Relations presented an intriguing model to help explain the relationship of commissioned workers to both the Office of the Public Ministry and the Priesthood of All Believers. Lehenbauer's model places the commissioned minister at the intersection of the "Office of Public Ministry Turnpike" and the "Royal Priesthood Parkway" (figure 9).

---

20 Klug, *Church and Ministry*, 268.

FIGURE 9

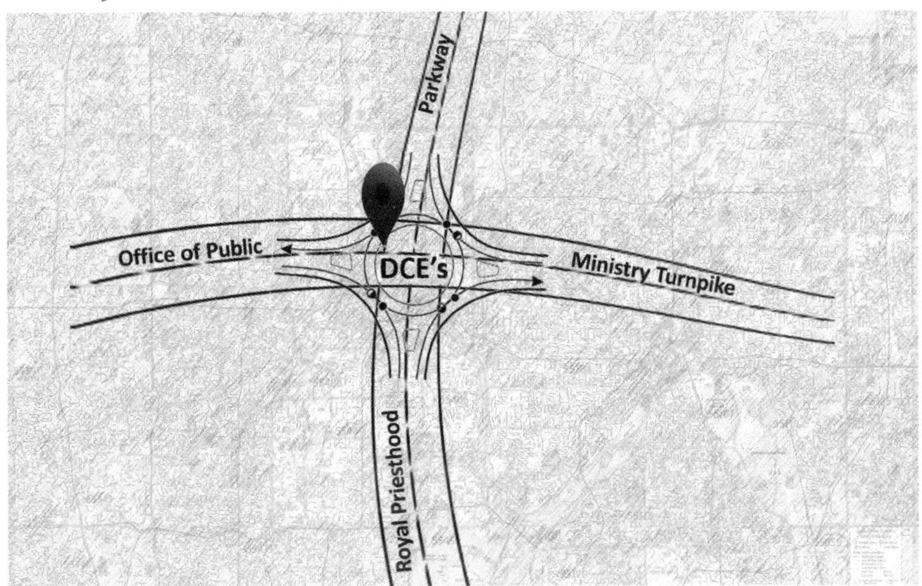

Presented by Dr. Joel Lehenbauer at the 2018 Heartland DCE Conference.

When considering the merits of this model, one must begin by keeping in mind that the goal of the model is not to separate those in public ministry from the Priesthood of All Believers. In explaining whether DCEs (and by extension all commissioned ministers) are in public ministry, he cites the CTCR 1981 report, which states:

> These are offices established by the church. Those who are called to serve in them are authorized to perform certain of the function(s) of the office of the public ministry. These offices are "ministry" and they are "public," yet they are not *the* office of the public ministry. Rather, they are auxiliary to that unique pastoral office, and those who hold these offices perform their assigned functions under the supervision of the holders of the pastoral office. Such offices are established by the churches as the need arises, and their specific functions are determined by the church.[21]

The distinction that the commissioned minister has a public ministry but is "not *the* office of public ministry" is a helpful distinction that merits further unpacking in subsequent chapters. Using the intersection model, the natural question is which road the commissioned minister is on. If one road relates to the pastoral office and the other to the laity, this statement further on in his presentation may be helpful.

21 Lehenbauer, *Equipping the Saints,* 15.

The holder of an auxiliary office may rejoice to say, "I am in the ministry" with a very specific meaning. He or she holds an office that is not only the priesthood of believers (which all Christians hold) nor the office of the public ministry. *It is a ministry that has its own validity.*[22]

CONCLUSION

The LCMS has had auxiliary offices since its founding. However, despite the nomenclature of the call used in reference to these offices, there have always been those in the LCMS who do not view the work of those in such auxiliary offices as properly ministry nor the people truly divinely called.

In order to address and seek to greater clarity with regard to this tension, subsequent chapters will walk through this theological and historical development of the Lutheran understanding of the Office of the Public Ministry.

---

22 Lehenbauer, *Equipping the Saints,* 24.

CHAPTER 3

Ministry from Luther to Gerhard

SETTING THE STAGE

In order to understand what it means today when we talk about the Office of the Public Ministry, it is important to consider how ministry was understood in the writings of our Lutheran forbearers, for it is upon the foundations they laid that the interpretive framework of Lutheranism has been established. It is critical to get a handle on how Luther, Chemnitz, and others approached Scripture in order to articulate a doctrine of the Office of the Public Ministry.

As already noted, the LCMS was founded with two types of called workers. There were pastors and there were teachers. Both were called, yet there was a clear distinction at work right from the beginning. Drawing on terminology from prior generations of Lutheran theologians, the office of the Lutheran teacher was considered an auxiliary office. The question however remains, what does it mean that an office is auxiliary? How does the auxiliary nature of these offices relate to the Office of the Public Ministry?

Francis Pieper, in his *Christian Dogmatics*, cites Luther as writing:

> For the office of preaching the Gospel is the highest among them all; for it is the true Apostolic office, laying the foundation of all other offices, on which it is proper to build all the others, namely, the offices of teacher, of prophet, of governors, of those who have the gift of healing.[1]

"Highest among them all." Does this imply multiple offices in the church? Marquart and others see auxiliary offices as something other than a part of the Office of the Public Ministry.

> When it comes to auxiliary offices, the classic example is of course that of the Seven in Acts 6:1–6. Although the noun "διάκονος" (deacon) is not used in this account, "διακονία" and the verb "διακονέω" (serve, esp. in connection with food, Lk. 10:40) are used (vv.1, 2). The office being created here is neither a new divinely instituted office, nor a specialization within the one office of the Gospel and sacraments. It is rather an auxiliary service established by the church in Christian liberty precisely to enable the one apostolic office of the Gospel . . . to devote itself to its proper work.[2]

---

1 Pieper, *Christian Dogmatics* (*Vol. 3*), 462.

2 Marquart, *The Church and Her Fellowship, Ministry, and Governance*, 140.

According to this line of thinking, while the church may be at liberty to establish additional offices, those offices ought not to be confused with the pastoral office. This works up to a point. While it is readily apparent that there would and should be concern over an equivocation in which the pastoral office is indistinguishable from other offices, to dismiss all other offices as he does seem inconsistent with many of the writings of our Lutheran church fathers.

> The church therefore may ask one of its public ministers of the Word to attend also to "tables," but a person commissioned only for the table-diakonia does not thereby become a public minister of the Gospel. In principle, this applies to all auxiliary offices, but in practice some of these offices presuppose that the incumbent is already in the public ministry, while others do not.[3]

Marquart here seems to argue that the deacons of Acts may have been excluded from the teaching ministry of the church. In part, this line of argumentation relies upon the theology of Gerhard.

Nispel offers some helpful distinctions and historical usage for terms that, he worries, are often misunderstood by English-speaking Lutherans in North America. He notes that the *Diakon* was understood as an ordained preacher who assisted the parish rector or *Pfarrherr*.[4] While Marquart might not argue that all deacons historically should be considered ordained, he, too, knows of some deacons as ordained preachers. His argument is that the word *deacon* in and of itself does not mean or necessarily include the sense of public minister of the Gospel.[5] It would seem that historical developments have indeed clouded our understanding of biblical as well as extrabiblical terminology.

Of further note is *Kirchendiener,* which Nispel explains as "a very general, broad, and abstract term used to refer to all offices and workers in the church together."[6] Nispel uses the term "church worker" as inclusive of both ordained and non-ordained, which may be called auxiliary. In order to examine these understandings of auxiliary ministry and provide clarity for using the term today, turning to Luther and his theological successors directly seems appropriate.

MARTIN LUTHER

Luther is a puzzle when it comes to trying to put together a picture of his view of the Office of the Public Ministry. Avoiding a hierarchical structure, typical to his style, Luther is not motivated to attempt to solidify his view of

---

3 Marquart, *The Church and Her Fellowship, Ministry, and Governance,* 141.

4 Nispel, "Pfarramt, Geography, and the Order of the Church," 243.

5 Marquart, *The Church and Her Fellowship, Ministry, and Governance,* 141.

6 Nispel, "Pfarramt, Geography, and the Order of the Church," 243.

ministry into a specific doctrinal statement.[7] This has allowed for an element of ambiguity to remain in the articulations of Lutheran theology in the writings of the generations of theological followers of Luther. More so, this has left possible the lack of clarity faced by those in auxiliary offices today.

F. V. N. Painter in *Luther on Education* notes that Luther held the teaching office in high esteem.[8] Further, he quotes Luther as having stated that "If I had to give up preaching and my other duties, there is no office I would rather have than that of school-teacher. For I know that next to the ministry it is the most useful, greatest, and best; and I am not sure which of the two is to be preferred."[9] This is high praise indeed. Here we see how Luther valued teaching of the faith, perhaps second only to the preaching of the Gospel.

Klug notes that

> It is especially in his treatise "Concerning the Ministry" of 1523 that Luther presses this great truth home. We are Christ's brethren "only because of the new birth," and not tonsures, long robes, and the like; nor by the "episcopal ordinations" under the aegis of the papal hierarchy; not by any other externals. The fact is that true priests before God are those by "birth," that is, by regeneration, by Baptism. And this makes the ministry of the Word something which "is common to all Christians," and this "highest office in the church" thus "belongs to all who are Christians, not only by right but by command." . . . Luther does not minimize the pastoral office itself and "the right and command to commit such office to a minster by vote of the congregation," but he contends eloquently for the Scriptural truth that its powers inhere first of all in the royal priesthood of believers whose duty it is under God to see to administrating of Word and Sacrament and to call qualified men into the preaching office.[10]

As much as Luther valued the teaching office, he placed the highest value on the preaching office. "When a pastor of the church is present, or any minister of the Word, and he cheers up this conscience, still, no matter how much it is cheered up, a groaning contrary to the will and all experience of consolation repeatedly returns."[11] Even as he makes the case for the preaching office, in a way Luther also makes the case for the ministry of auxiliary offices. For what else might it mean to juxtapose the ministry of the Word against other offices, if not to note there are other offices? Certainly, a citation such as this does not provide evidence as to Luther's position on the relation of these other offices

---

7 Jeffcoat, "Martin Luther's Doctrine of Ministry," 44.

8 Painter, *Luther on Education*, 142.

9 Painter, *Luther on Education*, 264.

10 Klug, "Luther on the Ministry," 298–99.

11 LW 6:371.

to the Office of the Public Ministry, but it speaks to their legitimate existence.

Klug explains how Luther understood the necessity for additional help for the local pastor in his ministry in cases where the congregation is large.

> In a busy and large parish, it might be necessary, Luther stated in a 1525 sermon, to divide it into four or five geographic parts, with various helpers assigned to assist the pastor in ministering to the soul and bodily needs of the parishioners. The primary responsibility, especially for the spiritual care, would reside in the called pastor; but we know from New Testament example, said Luther, that other helpers may be necessary, so that no one in the parish is neglected, body or soul. Such individual could rightly bear the name deacon or deaconess.[12]

In the context of ministry in sixteenth-century Germany, this may have been in reference to the ministerial assistance provided by deacons and subdeacons,[13] though there is question as to whether the deacon was given license to preach or merely to care for the souls of the community.[14]

Much of the effort made by Luther in articulating a doctrine of public ministry was in the context of the denigration of the ministry of the Word as seen in the Roman Catholic Church of his day. Schulz in his dissertation notes that this emphasis on the ministry of the Word is misapplied when used to suggest that the modern pastor is alone to be considered equivalent to the Office of the Public Ministry.[15] Schulz, writing on the relationship between pastors and teachers, is concerned that even the use of the term *auxiliary* denigrates the call of the teacher and other commissioned ministers.[16]

Rogness points out that the rapid growth of congregations in the fourth century necessitated the further development of the diaconate in support of the ministry of bishops and pastors. "Inevitably the diaconate as a separate office diminished in importance. During the Reformation era, Martin Luther favored the restoration of the diaconate to its original purpose, namely, to care for the poor and maintain church property."[17] Naumann notes that though Luther did not directly re-establish a female diaconate, he did however pave the way for its later development.[18]

---

12 Klug, *Church and Ministry,* 275.

13 Jeffcoat, "Martin Luther's Doctrine of Ministry," 47.

14 Jeffcoat, "Martin Luther's Doctrine of Ministry," 199.

15 Schulz, "Improving the Relationship between Pastor and Teacher in Light of the Doctrine of the Divine Call," 44.

16 Schulz, "Improving the Relationship between Pastor and Teacher," 44.

17 Rogness, "The Office of Deacon in the Christian Church," 155.

18 Naumann, *In the Footsteps of Phoebe,* 21–22.

In his 1523 work, *That a Christian Assembly or Congregation has the Right and Power to Judge All Teaching and to Call, Appoint, and Dismiss Teachers, Established and Proven by Scripture,* Luther discusses what he refers to as "lower offices."

> Therefore, whoever has the office of preaching imposed on him has the highest office in Christendom imposed on him. Afterward he may also baptize, celebrate mass, and exercise all pastoral care; or, if he does not wish to do so, he may confine himself to preaching and leave baptizing and other lower offices to others—as Christ and all the apostles did, Acts 4 [6:4].[19]

It is interesting that in this early work of Luther's, he seems to allow for a rather flexible approach to handling the work of pastoral ministry. While no one could argue that those without a call to preach as pastor to a local congregation should presume to do so, it seems that Luther was open to the local pastor allowing for those in lower offices to handle other elements of ministry, such as Baptism. What is less clear is if Luther here is assuming all such lower offices to be merely what we might term assistant or associate pastors. How this is understood by subsequent Lutheran theologians may shed light on Luther's own understanding.

MARTIN CHEMNITZ

Known as the second Martin, Chemnitz is credited by many as having preserved the original theology of Luther against the influence of the so-called Crypto-Calvinists. He was a key theologian and pastor during the second generation of the Reformation, and through his many theological writings and his contribution to the Formula of Concord brought into clearer focus the teachings that Luther had risked so much for during the generation prior.

> On the basis of New Testament teaching and examples, Martin Chemnitz subscribes fully to the position which Luther has articulated concerning the pastoral ministry as the highest and fundamental office ordained by God, and the auxiliary offices as arising from the need in the church for additional help.[20]

Chemnitz, as Klug notes, consistent with his larger work solidifying the theological work of Luther, solidifies Luther's understanding of the Office of the Public Ministry as well. Again, we see an emphasis on the pastoral office along with the assisting ministry of the auxiliary offices.

Chemnitz offers a rather pragmatic explanation of the necessity in some situations for the pastor to be assisted in the fulfilling of his office by others.

---

19 LW 39:314.

20 Klug, *Church and Ministry,* 276.

> The fact of the matter is this: Because many duties belong to the ministry of the church which cannot all conveniently be performed by one person or by a few, when the believers are very numerous—in order, therefore, that all things may be done in an orderly way, decently, and for edification, these duties of the ministry began, as the assembly of the church grew great, to be distributed among a certain ranks of ministers which they afterward called *taxeis* (ranks) or *tagmata* (orders), so that each might have, as it were, a certain designated station in which he might serve the church in certain duties of the ministry.[21]

Notice that not only does Chemnitz point out the necessity for assistance for the work of the pastor, but he refers to this work as "duties of the ministry." He goes on to stress "that for the welfare of the assembly of the church the individual duties which belong to the ministry might be attended to more conveniently, rightly, diligently, and orderly, with a measure of dignity and for edification"[22] as the rationale for the introduction of such orders or ranks. He points back to the apostles as having begun this necessary division of the labor of ministry. Chemnitz's phrasing clearly indicates that those in lower ranks were still to be considered ministers. There is no dismissive attempt to distinguish between "true ministry" and supporting ministry through other work (waiting tables). Rather, Chemnitz seems comfortable discussing the need for these additional ranks of ministers as ministers by virtue of their appointment.

Chemnitz stresses that there is no command in God's Word for these orders. There is no specific list or required number or type. They are to be established for the sake of "good order, decorum, and edification"[23] in the church. "These ranks . . . were not something besides and beyond the ministry of the Word and sacraments, but the real and true duties of the ministry were distributed among certain ranks for the reasons already set forth."[24] For Chemnitz, the need for these additional ranks was based on the size of the local congregation and the needs of that congregation that could not be adequately cared for by a single pastor. Whether these additional ranks included the need of additional pastoral ministry or ranks focused on specific needs within the general pastoral care of the faithful, the local church had Christian freedom to engage these servants in the ministry of the church.

21 Chemnitz, *Examination of the Council of Trent: Part II*, 682–83.

22 Chemnitz, *Examination of the Council of Trent: Part II*, 683.

23 Chemnitz, *Examination of the Council of Trent: Part II*, 685.

24 Chemnitz, *Examination of the Council of Trent: Part II*, 685.

At the same time, the freedom of the church to formulate these additional ranks or offices is stressed. For Klug points out that Chemnitz supported this understanding with the clear teaching of Scripture that "We have not command of God which sets such offices, or various ranks, like bishops, etc., in the church, but only the one office, the public pastoral ministry."[25] Thus, despite talking about ranks, Chemnitz was not seeking to establish a hierarchical system.

> The apostles at first embraced within their persons and office all the duties pertaining to the care and nurture of their flocks, and only as their congregations grew and it became humanly impossible for them to fulfill all the needs of their parishes did they, for the sake of the congregation's welfare, parcel out some of the functions which were auxiliary to their ministry to others, carefully chosen individuals who qualified as servants of God and enjoyed the esteem of their fellow believers.[26]

Now it may be argued that just because Chemnitz can be seen to support the establishment of these additional offices, this does not necessarily justify the inclusion of those offices as a part of the Office of the Public Ministry. Further, the performing of the functions of what might typically be a part of the pastoral office does not make one a minister. True enough, but that does not appear to be the line of thinking used by Chemnitz at this point.

What seems more likely to be the case from the context is that Chemnitz is providing a distinction. The Office of the Public Ministry is first and foremost exercised through the Office of the Pastor. However, rather than merely stopping there, Chemnitz suggests by his use of terms like *ranks* and *auxiliary* that the Office of the Public Ministry may also be exercised through ministers who do not hold the Office of the Pastor. Said differently, while the Office of the Public Ministry always involves a pastor, it can involve other sorts of ministers depending on the particular needs of the church within the context that the ministry of the church is taking place. Thus the size of a congregation as well as the cultural and social needs of ministry may, if not should, be cause to institute additional offices called as Ministers of the Word to support the ministry of the Office of the Pastor. Given this schema, a high view of the Office of the Pastor as the sole office instituted by Christ and required as a part of the ministry of the church remains, while allowing an appropriate place for the ministry of other helping offices designed by the church to further the ministry.

It would not do to see these additional offices as a part of the ministry merely due to the function that they fulfill. It would instead be more natural to argue that these offices are established by a formal act of the church itself. The

---

25 Klug, *Church and Ministry*, 277.

26 Klug, *Church and Ministry*, 277.

service of the seven in Acts 6 did not qualify them for an office in the public ministry, but the public placement of them by the church in that office.

In volume 9 of Chemnitz's works on *Church Order,* he discusses the placement of the schoolmaster as follows:

> Therefore, at whatsoever time a schoolmaster or assistant is nominated or presented to our church councillors by our officers and courts of each district, according to their provenance, or when, in the search made by our officers and courts, one of our church councillors is called or one offers his service himself, each one shall, before being admitted into the examination, present to our church councils credible and lawful testimony and documentation about his origin, education, person, and life, either from the authorities under whom he previously dwelt during his service, education, and life ... If he then is found qualified, especially in grammar, he shall next be examined in an orderly fashion and with special diligence by our church councillor with regard to his piety, on the basis of our Catechism as included in our church ordinances.[27]

Notice the manner in which candidates for schoolmaster were examined according to the doctrinal standards of Lutheranism. Just as Lutheran pastors are expected to subscribe to the Lutheran confessions, so to all church workers are to serve in accord with Lutheran teaching.[28]

DAVID CHYTRAEUS

A contemporary of Chemnitz as well as fellow student of Melanchthon, David Chytraeus may also provide for us a bit of insight into the nature of the Office of the Public Ministry. In his work *On Sacrifice,* Chytraeus emphasizes that the individual member of the Body of Christ is not by one's own authority able to enter into the public ministry. It is rather within the context of the call from the Body of Christ that those individuals called by God to serve the church are placed into their office.

> For necessary to the public execution of the priestly office of instructing, consoling, exhorting, denouncing sins, judging controversies over doctrine, etc., is a thorough knowledge of Christian theology, a faculty for teaching, skill in languages, speaking ability, and other gifts, and these are not equally manifest in all whom the Holy Spirit has regenerated; therefore, those who lack these talents rightly yield their privileges to others better endowed than themselves.[29]

---

27 Chemnitz, *Church Order for Braunschweig-Wolfenbüttel,* 231–32.

28 Chemnitz, *Church Order,* 232.

29 Chytraeus, *On Sacrifice,* 98.

As has been illustrated above, the public nature of the ministry is what is distinguished from the general priesthood. Note, too, that for Chytraeus there is a yielding that takes place. Those members neither suited nor called to serve in public ministry should with joy empower, as a part of the local congregation, the public ministry of those with the calling, skill, and training to do so on their behalf and in the stead of Christ. To state this another way, those not called into public ministry should uplift and empower those who are called into ministry.

In a similar manner as others explain the development of ranks or offices within the ministry, Chytraeus asserts that

> Later, by human authority, ranks were established among the ministers and bishops, and within the presbyterate there appeared the ostiary, the psalmist, the lector, the exorcist, the acolyte, the subdeacon, the deacon, and the priest. One bishop – or overseer, or superintendent – was placed in charge of many presbyters or pastors of individual churches.[30]

Notice that these ranks are described as established ministers. There is no attempt made here to distinguish between the various offices, which are to be seen as ministers and which are merely serving in support of those who are in proper public ministry. The list includes many offices that are rather foreign to our modern ears. The church, then as now, is called to respond to the context in which it serves in order to best distribute the needed functions of ministry into offices that uplift the overall ministry of the church and support the ministry of the local pastor.

Wisely, Chytraeus offers both a further affirmation of the ranks or offices of ministry, along with a caution for their abuse.

> This episcopal order and the ranks connected with it are not evil in themselves. They should not be disparaged when they serve to uphold the unity and harmony of the church in true evangelical doctrine and the preservation of Christian discipline and peace; when they maintain and spread right doctrine and reverent worship of God; when they do not claim that they possess the illicit power to interpret Scripture arbitrarily, to establish new articles of faith, to legislate in matters of doctrine and worship; and when they do not assume tyrannical authority over the other members of the church, etc.[31]

The Christian liberty to establish additional offices to support the ministry of the pastoral office does not give license for just any functions of ministry to be shared. As an example, Chytraeus notes that this liberty does not give those entrusted with these offices the freedom to arbitrarily interpret the Scriptures.

---

30 Chytraeus, *On Sacrifice*, 100.

31 Chytraeus, *On Sacrifice*, 101–2.

JOHANN GERHARD

Prolific in his writing, Johann Gerhard's Theological Commonplaces are currently becoming far more accessible to the English-speaking world. What does this theologian of Lutheranism's age of orthodoxy have to offer to this discussion of the Office of the Public Ministry?

Klug states that "Gerhard chimes in with Chemnitz that ranks or orders among the clergy do not rest on the authority of God's Word, nor on apostolic precedent."[32] In his work on ecclesiastical ministry, Gerhard discusses the work of deacons, especially as described by Paul in Romans.

> Second, it is attributed to the *ecclesiastical order,* and this, again, in different ways; (a) Preeminently, it is attributed to *Christ,* who is the chief Shepherd and, by His own ministry on earth, has consecrated and sanctified the ecclesiastical ministry . . . (b) In a more general sense it is attributed to *all ministers of the church,* who serve God and the church by teaching, administering the Sacraments, and performing other duties of the ecclesiastical ministry . . . (c) In a more specific sense, it is taken to mean those who were occupied chiefly with that duty of the ecclesiastical ministry that involves food and distribution of necessities.[33]

Here it should be noted that Gerhard appears to include the ministry of deacons along with other ecclesiastical offices as properly ministries of the church. The source of all ministry is in the authority of Christ. Gerhard refers to Christ as our chief Shepherd. Within the context of the local church, the pastor serves as undershepherd in the stead and by the command of Christ. Those in auxiliary offices serve under the ministry of these undershepherds placed there by the local congregation.

Coming back to the claim of Gerhard's belief that the deacons of Acts were excluded from the teaching ministry of the church,[34] a different picture is painted in Gerhard's own words here as he discusses Romans 16:

> This seems to mean especially a ministry to the sick, but nothing prevents it from meaning, in general, the care of the sick, and travelers. You see, v. 2 follows with: "For she has been a patroness [προστάτις] of many, and of myself as well," [that is,] "she has given hospitality to many" and expended her efforts generously for their needs. The apostle explains how such deaconesses should be tested and selected before they are received into the ministries of the church (1 Tim. 5:9–10). But in the end those deacons were commissioned also with the ordinary duty of teaching (from which

---

32 Klug, *Church and Ministry,* 277.

33 Gerhard, *On the Ministry I,* 39.

34 Marquart, *The Church and Her Fellowship, Ministry, and Governance,* 140.

> also those whom Acts 6 mentions were not simply excluded, though they were chiefly in charge of the tables), so that they, joined to the presbyters, preached the Word together with them, administered the Sacraments, visited the sick, etc. In this way, they were made teachers of a lower order in the church.[35]

If this is an indication of a separate commissioning to teach, which may be a right understanding, what then is meant by their being teachers of a lower order? It might be that Gerhard is here indicating a similar status as we might see in our modern nomenclature of assistant or associate pastors. However, is this the only possible meaning behind his words?

Might it be that rather than being ordained as pastors in order to carry out the teaching ministry of the church, that these deacons were simply entrusted with this task as an addition to their previous diaconal duties? This latter interpretation of Gerhard can be supported by his own words later in the same book when he states that "it is false to say that the deacons had been put in charge merely of tables, for we have shown earlier from the example of Stephen and Philip that they, too, performed the teaching office."[36] Further, in the second volume of his work on ecclesiastical ministry, Gerhard notes:

> There are two kinds of *deacons*, so called from "ministering." Some were in charge of the care of the poor and the management of the church property.... One the other hand, some had been joined to the bishops or presbyters in the office of teaching and of administering the Sacraments in order to take their place and alleviate their labors.[37]

Here we see Gerhard distinguish between two kinds of deacons. Not all deacons were called to teach or administer the sacraments. This speaks to the church's use of Christian liberty to call ministers to a variety of roles of ministry. Yet, how are we to understand deacons who administer the sacraments? Does this not imply that deacons would have been ordained or at least understood as ordained pastors are today rather than commissioned ministers? As noted above, the use of the term *deacon* may be both those entrusted to preach and those entrusted with other areas of service.[38]

The authority of the Office of the Public Ministry is clearly seen in Gerhard as having been given by Christ to the pastoral office. It can also be seen in Gerhard that the role of the deacon, and by implication other auxiliary offices, is to support the ministry of the pastoral office.

---

35 Gerhard, *On the Ministry I,* 40.

36 Gerhard, *On the Ministry I,* 131.

37 Gerhard, *On the Ministry II,* 47.

38 Marquart, *The Church and Her Fellowship, Ministry, and Governance,* 141.

THE LUTHERAN CONFESSIONS

Having examined individual theologians of the Reformation era, this final section of the chapter will examine how the Lutheran reformers codified their views on ministry in the Lutheran Confessions. Robert Kolb notes that the development and use of confessions as a way to define the church was a new way of thinking.[39] This new use of the term was necessary to help clarify the confession of faith as understood by the Lutheran reformers as opposed to the teaching of the Roman Catholic Church, as well as the confessions being articulated by those in other branches of Protestantism that were forming at that time.

Article V of the Augsburg Confession declares that

> So that we may obtain this faith, the ministry of teaching the Gospel and administrating the Sacraments was instituted. Through the Word and Sacraments, as through instruments, the Holy Spirit is given [John 20:22]. He works faith, when and where it pleases God [John 3:8], in those who hear the good news that God justifies those who believe that they are received into grace for Christ's sake. This happens not through our own merits, but for Christ's sake.
>
> Our churches condemn the Anabaptists and others who think that through their own preparations and works the Holy Spirit comes to them without the external Word.[40]

The preaching office (*Predigtamt*) is not instituted by man. This divine office is necessary for the church in order that the Gospel is rightly taught and the Sacraments are rightly administered. This article is included not merely to explicate the nature of what ministry is and who ministers are to be, but rather to address how faith is obtained.[41]

Rejected here is any notion that individuals may take it upon themselves to declare that they are able to hear from God apart from the means instituted by God, namely God's Word and Sacraments. God works through means and has stated as much. In Galatians 1:8, Paul warns that even if he were to teach a gospel contrary to what he had already preached to them, the church in Galatia was to reject that teaching as false. Thus the final rule and norm for teaching can only be found in Scripture alone.

Further, the Lutheran Confessions note:

> Out of His immense goodness and mercy, God provides for the public preaching of His divine eternal Law and His wonderful plan for our re-

---

39 Kolb, *The Way of Concord*, 18.

40 AC V.

41 Beck, *The Doctrine of Faith*, 92.

> demption, that of the holy, only saving Gospel of His eternal Son, our only Savior and Redeemer, Jesus Christ. By this preaching He gathers an eternal Church for Himself from the human race and works in people's hearts true repentance, knowledge of sins, and true faith in God's Son, Jesus Christ.[42]

Thus the preaching office is the instrument by which God calls together the church, cares for it, calls it to correction, and ultimately brings the gathered faithful unto salvation.

When the church is called and gathered by the Holy Spirit through the ministry of the preaching office, "Our churches teach that no one should publicly teach in the Church, or administer the Sacraments, without a rightly ordered call."[43] Just as individual Christians are not to take it upon themselves to claim an alternate source for normative teaching, so too individual Christians are not to take it upon their own authority to publicly teach or administer the Sacraments. It is rather the church that places individuals into the Office of Public Ministry.

In context, this article speaks against self-appointed authority and does not directly address the question of auxiliary offices. Instead, here and elsewhere in the Lutheran Confessions, the reformers were dealing with other concerns such as the authority of bishops.[44] Where bishops and pastors are given authority, the Augsburg Confession Article XXVIII notes "that it is lawful for bishops, or pastors, to make ordinances so that things will be done orderly in the Church, but not to teach that we merit grace or make satisfaction for sins."[45] In context, this article is dealing with distinguishing the authority of the bishop in both the secular and sacred realms.

The balance of AC XXVIII seeks to distinguish the authority of the church from the authority of the government. The power of the church and the power of the state each play their role in God's economic rule; however, one ought not to confuse the two. Is then the ministry of those who serve in non-church organizations properly to be considered ministry? Is not a similar mistake being made in according the Lutheran teacher a sacred ministry for a secular task? A similar argument might be offered for those pastors who serve non-church organizations and whose primary work is not focused around Word and Sacrament. Pastors in the LCMS are not removed from the roster for working at our publishing house, universities, or RSOs. Despite their work being beyond the central focus on ministry on Word and Sacrament, they serve connecting

---

42 SD II 50.

43 AC XIV.

44 See Ap XIV; AC XXVIII.

45 AC XXVIII 53.

this ministry with the particular area of work. Likewise, the Lutheran teacher who does not teach exclusively theology is no less in ministry when teaching math or science. Their theological training and spiritual care for their students comes to bear at all times in their ministry.

Can we say then that the Lutheran Confessions allow for the calling of auxiliary ministers? Robert Preus answers no. Having examined the Confessions, Preus provides a list of forms of service to the church that he deems unworthy of being called ministry. Arguing rightly that there is but one ministry, Preus lists military service, social work, accounting, and church administration among other roles that are not to be considered for a call to ministry. Interestingly, in the midst of this list Preus includes Directors of Christian Education, referring to them as "so-called."[46]

The list includes evangelist, which was considered for inclusion by the LCMS as a called office. Otherwise the balance of those itemized are much more clearly not ministry related. Rather than solidifying his argument, this enumeration works to reveal a lack of understanding related to the service of the DCE.

The principle author of the Augsburg Confession, Philip Melanchthon, has been at times argued to have preached and administered the sacraments. This is however not the case.[47] Yet, not merely in the writing of the Augsburg Confession, Melanchthon taught and trained future and current ministers. This public confession was a ministry service that he rendered with skill. Whether he or anyone at that time would have considered him akin to our modern commissioned ministers is not easily determined.

What can be said, however, is that in context the Lutheran Confessions were dealing with and attempting to provide clarity to different questions than those posed in this book. The reformers were articulating the necessity of the preaching office, the proper authority necessary to place one into said office, and the distinction in authority between the church and the state, as well as between the local pastor/congregation and the bishop.

Kolb points out that it is not possible for all biblical teaching to be covered in a single book.[48] This does not negate the rightful claim that the Lutheran Confessions are foundational to right Lutheran teaching. It does however, speak to the need for further consideration as new questions and situations arise.

SUMMARY

Our Lutheran forbearers held a very high view of the Office of the Public

---

46 Preus, *The Doctrine of the Call in the Confessions and Lutheran Orthodoxy*, 16.

47 Piepkorn et al., *The Church: Selected Writings of Arthur Carl Piepkorn*, vol. 1, 74.

48 Kolb, *The Way of Concord*, 89.

Ministry. That ought not to be lost in any discussion of the current nature of that office. Luther sought to restore the role of the pastor from the priestly morass of Medieval Romanism. That was the context of much of his writing on the subject.

Yet at the same time, in the writings of these Lutheran theologians one is able to discern not merely a high view of the ministry of the pastor, but the freedom for the church to augment this ministry as the early church did when deacons were established. There is a place in their thinking not only for the ministry of the pastor but for the participation of other servants of the Word.

This does not yet answer the questions specifically related to the place of commissioned ministers in relation to the Office of the Public Ministry. To move closer to our contemporary situation, the next chapter will turn to C. F. W. Walther and his conception of the ministry formed during the tumultuous time leading up to the founding of the LCMS.

CHAPTER 4

Ministry in the Theology of Walther

SAXON IMMIGRATION

With C. F. W. Walther, our study of Lutheran theologians on this matter comes closer to home in the LCMS. Walther was one of the principal figures in the founding of the LCMS, having taken up key leadership at a time of great struggle among a group of Saxon immigrants. An assessment of Walther's understanding of the doctrine of ministry would be lacking if some comment is not made with regard to the context in which he found his leadership.

Having arrived in America from Germany, a group of Saxon immigrants found themselves first in New Orleans. Then, traveling up the Mississippi, they settled nearby St. Louis in Perry County. This group of faithful and confessional Lutherans undertook the perils of this journey in order that they might preserve the Lutheran faith in the confessional form as handed down to them. They rightly resisted the rationalism that was currently in vogue in the universities and church schools of Saxony. They were concerned that this rationalism would undermine faith in the Scriptures and weaken the confessional distinctions between the Reformed and Lutheran. They were concerned that the distinctive nature of confessional Lutheran theology would be lost, mingled with Reformed practice and theology, which was at odds with their understanding of theology and the practice of worship.

Martin Stephan organized a group of 707 people who set sail for the new world on five ships in 1838. Four of those ships with 602 passengers from the original group arrived in New Orleans in January 1839. Continuing up the Mississippi, a portion of this group settled in St. Louis itself, while the majority elected to establish their new home in the hills of Perry County.

The story of the fall of Martin Stephan is a complicated and controversial one. Stephan was noted as a strong, perhaps dictatorial leader. When accusations of sexual misconduct and mismanagement of funds surfaced, these Saxon immigrants, who risked a great deal in following him to America, quite literally sent him away across the river, exiling him across the Mississippi to Illinois.

In this context, Walther was elevated to the leadership and pastoral headship of this new community. One of the early concerns that surfaced focused on the theology of the call and the Office of the Public Ministry. Without Stephan, the forefathers of the LCMS were isolated. Stephan had served as their bishop prior to his ousting. No longer under his leadership, the Saxons were uncertain that they had the authority to ordain pastors to provide for the ongoing ministry of their immigrant community. Without a bishop, they did not have a formal connection to the church back in Germany, from which to request pastors ordained by bishops in Germany. How were they to provide pastors and teachers for the ongoing ministry of the church in America? As their community grew, would they be able to and did they have the right to provide workers for the church through means devised and established themselves?

Through his studies of Scripture and Luther, Walther came to argue that the right to call, and in fact to ordain, pastors rested in the local congregation and not in the external authority of a bishop via apostolic succession. The church, in the absence of a bishop, was perfectly within its theological rights to call both a new bishop and new pastors to serve its people. Though they received a good many pastors through the years for Germany through the efforts of men like Wilhelm Löhe, the authority of the call was not his to grant, but the local churches. A church body, such as the LCMS, may as a gathered group of local churches establish training criteria for pastors based on the scriptural qualifications for the office, as they would in the years to come, but the authority of the call rested in the local church.

FORMATION OF THE SYNOD

As Walther worked to solidify what would become the LCMS through the establishment of churches, he also worked tirelessly on the establishment of educational institutions to support the ministry of the church. Building on the strong connection between church and school in their homeland, the founders of the LCMS placed a great emphasis on the establishment of schools. At times, the school was opened even before the church was planted.

Naturally, along with the establishment of schools came the necessity of having well-trained and theologically faithful teachers. Many times, these early teachers were pastors called to plant the church. However, as the task of managing both roles became too burdensome, other men who were trained and specifically called to teach were needed.[1] As the system of schools grew and the number of teachers increased, Walther was repeatedly called upon or believed it incumbent upon himself to offer some teaching on the relationship between the pastor and the teacher.

> This was the picture or image which the Lutheran forefathers, like Walther and his colleagues, envisioned for the pastoral office in its relationship to the other offices established within the congregation, or within the synod. As from one main stream at its delta, the tributaries flowed in the direction called for by the pastoral office and its God-given functions.

---

1 Kretzmann, *A Brief History of Education,* 113.

> If the figure or image of the tree be used, the pastoral office itself is understood to be the trunk, from which the auxiliaries branch off according to need.[2]

Thus the Lutheran teacher was considered by Walther to have a call derived from the call of the pastor. This seems natural considering the way in which teachers were called to take up a function that became too much for the local pastor to handle and still apply all the necessary time, energy, and study to his primary call to serve the congregation in preaching and teaching in that context.

This should strike the reader as similar to what took place in Acts 6, when the apostles set aside seven men to serve the widows. The apostles recognized that their preaching and evangelization work was beginning to suffer as they had less and less time to dedicate to those efforts. The widows were worthy of service, but was it for the apostles to do? The rationale and meaning of what the apostles did when they set aside the seven for this service to the widows—and, more to the point, the larger church—will be examined in greater detail later on.

Picking up the terminology explored previously, Walther discussed the role of the Lutheran teacher as an auxiliary ministry.

> When Walther terms these supportive offices "merely a part of the office of the ministry," he in no way denigrates them, nor speaks lightly of them. This could hardly be his intent, for he closes his comments with the asseveration that they "are all to be regarded as sacred offices of the Church," simply by virtue of their rootage.[3]

Walther held Lutheran teachers in high esteem. For him, the use of the term *auxiliary* was not an insult. This was not a way to denigrate or place a less value upon their work. There was a balance to the way Walther understood auxiliary ministry.

In an article originally published in German in 1932 and subsequently translated for publication in English in 1989, Kretzmann notes the following:

> In Acts 6 we read of special almoners who were elected and installed by the congregation to meet a special emergency. It almost seems as if the office of these men was terminated at the dispersion of the congregation after the death of Stephen; for we find one of them, Philip, as an evangelist at Caesarea in the year 58 (Acts 21:8). However, the fact that the office of elder persisted and that these men later again took over the function

---

2 Klug, *Church and Ministry,* 269.

3 Klug, *Church and Ministry,* 271.

> of the almoners seems apparent from Acts 11:30. An office similar to that of the almoners in Jerusalem was that of the deacons somewhat later, of whom we hear in 1 Timothy 3:8–10, 12, 13.[4]

Setting aside the argument that Kretzmann makes that Stephen and the others were almoners and not deacons, it is helpful to acknowledge the occasional manner in which the church established auxiliary offices. Kretzmann explicitly expresses this when he states, "Thus we have an indication that under given circumstances and conditions we can also place special gifts of grace in the service of that congregation, namely by *creating auxiliary offices* that provide ancillary services for the pastorate."[5]

Kretzmann further notes that "we must not forget that the *qualifications* prescribed in Scripture for incumbents of the pastorate are, all other things being equal, *also in force for the incumbents of all the auxiliary office* (e.g., the 'apt to teach' for all teachers), as well as that by means of such auxiliary offices the duties of the pastor as the guardian of souls can of course be diminished but not be set aside."[6] There are times when it may seem as if lifting up the ministry of auxiliary offices has a negative impact on the view of the pastoral office in the church. Walther had no such concern. Walther held to a high view of both the pastoral office and the auxiliary office of the teacher. While there were restrictions to the ministry of the Lutheran teacher that would not apply to the pastor, even a pastor teaching in the school, this did not mean that the office entrusted to the teacher was seen as a lesser office.

Walther held that the church is obligated to establish the office of the pastor. Though the power and authority to proclaim the Word of God and to administer the Sacraments belongs to all believers, according to Walther, the church transfers this authority to the bearer of the pastoral office. Thus the pastor proclaims God's Word and administers the sacraments on behalf of the church. The pastoral office is the highest office of the church. Auxiliary offices may be created by the church to serve and support the ministry of the pastoral office, but they are branches of the pastoral office. They are bearers of a part of the public ministry only. Auxiliary office bearers are not entrusted with the full Office of the Public Ministry, as Wohlrabe, in his review of Walther's teaching, concludes, that auxiliary office bearers are not entrusted with the full Office of the Public Ministry.[7] The authority for the ministry of these auxiliary offices derives from the congregation but flows through the pastoral office.

Notice that there are a couple of key things going on in Wohlrabe's dis-

---

4 Kretzmann, "Apostolate, Preaching Ministry, Pastorate, Synodical Office," 269.

5 Kretzmann, "Apostolate, Preaching Ministry," 270.

6 Kretzmann, "Apostolate, Preaching Ministry," 271.

7 Wohlrabe, "An Historical Analysis of the Doctrine of the Ministry in The Lutheran Church—Missouri Synod," 11.

cussion of Walther on ministry. First, the authority of the ministry rests in the hands of the Priesthood of All Believers. As the Body of Christ, gathered as a local church, each member of the Priesthood of All Believers holds the authority for ministry of Word and Sacrament. Walther saw in this an understanding that helped the LCMS establish its seminaries and colleges to raise up and train church workers. If the local church is the body that has the authority to issue the call, then churches gathered together in a synod, affirming the scriptural qualifications for ministry, would possess the authority to establish criteria by which church workers are to be trained.

Second, it should be noted that individual members of the priesthood do not have the authority to exercise these functions of ministry publicly. Rather, the church corporately places men into office to serve and execute the office. Third, the church is able, as it had done in Acts and with the Lutheran teacher, to establish auxiliary offices and place people to serve in those offices.

Notice that Walther saw these auxiliary office bearers as "partakers of the public office of the ministry. However, they did not have the full office of ministry."[8] Walther many times and in a variety of settings and publications affirmed this position. However, he does not fully unpack what it means to partake in only a part of the Office of the Public Ministry. This lack of clarification has lingered in the theological discussions on the office of ministry in the LCMS since his time.

What is certain in Walther's assessment of auxiliary offices is that they should be recognized as sacred offices. These auxiliary offices have a place within the one Office of the Public Ministry. These auxiliary offices aid the ministry of the pastor in preaching the Word.[9] This articulation of Walther's position as found in *The Voice of Our Church on the Question of Church and Ministry* was officially adopted by the LCMS in 1851. Wohlrabe goes on to note that in *Pastoral Theology* Walther insisted that the divine office of the teacher is not to be forgotten. "As heavy a cross as it is for a preacher and as much as the work of God is necessarily hindered if he has schoolteacher against him, he has just as glorious a support in him if he is pulling on one yoke with him in true unity of spirit."[10] This branch office of the pastoral office is to be held in high esteem by the pastor as he works with the teacher. They are to function as colleagues in ministry.[11] Sadly all too often this is forgotten or simply rejected outright.

Not only is this forgotten in a practical sense in the regular work of the local church, but subsequent theologians have been far from a consistent source of affirmation of Walther's position. For example, Francis Pieper understood the

---

8 Wohlrabe, "An Historical Analysis," 11.

9 Wohlrabe, "An Historical Analysis," 61.

10 Walther, *Pastoral Theology*, 463.

11 Wohlrabe, "An Historical Analysis," 64.

doctrine of the ministry in a similar way to Walther's understanding; however, differences are found in their understanding of auxiliary offices. Pieper does not discuss auxiliary offices as divine. The pastoral office alone and specifically the office of the local church pastor is noted as divine in Pieper. An example of Pieper's treatment of the subject can be see when he cites Luther:

> If the office of the Word is conferred on a man, there are conferred on him all offices which are administered in the Church through the Word, such as the power to baptize, to bless, [bread and wine, administer Communion, St. L. X:1576], to bind and to loose, to pray, to examine, or judge.[12]

This in no way means that he can be seen as denying the right of the local church or church body to create necessary auxiliary offices. He merely does not refer to them as divine in origin.[13] As noted previously, Pieper's citation of Luther continues by placing the office of preaching as the highest office, separating this office from the rest. Though not a direct endorsement of auxiliary offices, room is present for their existence in support of the pastoral office.

This is the very situation that this current work is focused upon. All too often our theologians talk in terms of clergy and laity, but they fail to offer a solid home in either category for the commissioned minister. Those in auxiliary ministry often find it difficult to see how they properly fit in either. Unlike the laity, commissioned ministers are called by churches and schools. Yet, this does not make them clergy.

Wohlrabe further notes that just as pastors offer a pledge of confessional fidelity, "Walther stated that everything which had been said concerning pastors also applied to the teachers. They were in a church office, called to teach the Word of God."[14] With that call to teach comes an examination of the theological understanding of those who would do so. All commissioned ministers have minimum theological standards to complete with respect to course work as well as an examination prior to certification and commissioning to join the roster. While the course work is not equivalent for a Director of Parish Music and a pastor, they are both asked to make the same pledge.

CHURCH AND MINISTRY

In his classic work *The Church and the Office of the Ministry*, Walther in Thesis VIII states that "The preaching office [*Predigtamt*] is the highest office in the Church, from which flow all other offices in the Church."[15] Expounding upon this thesis, Walther notes that the pastoral office "must of necessity be the

---

12 Pieper, *Christian Dogmatics* (Vol. 2), 462.

13 Wohlrabe, "An Historical Analysis," 156.

14 Wohlrabe, "An Historical Analysis," 64.

15 Walther, *The Church and the Office of the Ministry*, 284.

highest in the Church, and all other offices flow from it. For the Keys embrace the whole authority of the Church."[16] In the highest office, Walther includes "elders, bishops, rulers, stewards, etc." while he calls those not in this higher office "deacons." This is not to say that there is but one office of deacon, but to connect the nature of auxiliary offices to the establishment of deacons by the apostles.

As noted above, the apostles recognized the need to add to and diversify those who served the growing church. "Hence at Jerusalem the holy apostles in the beginning administered not only the preaching office but also the office of deacon until the growth of the congregation demanded that this office should be conferred on particular persons in order to support the first office."[17] When the church is able to be cared for by a single pastor, wonderful. When there is a need for an additional pastor, the church ought to call one. When the needs of the congregation call for a greater diversity of servants, then simply calling another pastor would actually be a disservice, as the church is then not being provided for according to need.

Notice that the listing of names associated with the highest office is longer than the single name of deacon provided as an auxiliary office. Scripture makes use of a number of terms that we today consider to be part of what we call the pastoral office. While we have a greater emphasis today on the singular nature of the pastoral office, we have our own set of diverse terminology. Whether one is a senior, sole, or associate pastor, all are pastors. Additionally, district and synodical presidents are still considered pastors.

We have expounded upon the concept of the deacon, and rather than organizing around the nomenclature of deacon, the LCMS has established a number of director positions (see chapter 1) as a part of the larger number of auxiliary or commissioned offices. Other Lutheran church bodies have addressed this in different ways.

Walther continues by explaining how the church is able to establish auxiliary offices.

> Hence the highest office is that of the preaching office, with which all other offices are also conferred at the same time. Every other public office in the church is part of the same, or a helping office [*Hilfsamt*] that stands at the side of the preaching office, whether it be the office of elder([possessors of which] do not labor in the Word and doctrine [1 Timothy 5:17]) or the ruling office [*Regieramt*] (Romans 12:8) or the deaconate (the office of service in a narrow sense) or whatever other offices the church may entrust to particular persons for special administration. Therefore,

---

16 Walther, *The Church and the Office of the Ministry*, 285.

17 Walther, *The Church and the Office of the Ministry*, 285–86.

> the offices of [Christian day] schoolteachers who have to teach the Word of God in their schools, distributors of alms, sextons, precentors at public worship, and others are all to be regarded as churchly, holy offices, which bear a part of the one church office, stand at the side (for they take over a part of the one church office) and stand beside the preaching office.[18]

Here the list of auxiliary offices is far larger. Walther offers examples of auxiliary offices established and utilized over the course of the centuries by the church. There is no expectation that these are permanent offices. Only the pastoral office is such a permanent office. Auxiliary offices, rather, are established to deal with a particular need and grounded in the particular context in which the church has found itself throughout centuries. All, however, are to be considered divine.

With its emphasis on educational ministry through the local Lutheran schools, the LCMS was immediately in need of an office of Lutheran teacher. This has not waned. Rather, the church has instead developed additional auxiliary offices in order to address the evolving needs presented by the ministry of the church in our culture.

The source for all these offices is a single office, that of the Office of the Public Ministry. This ought to continually remind those who serve in auxiliary offices, not of their lesser station, but rather how to align their own ministry.

> Walther had this in mind, when in the second part of the same thesis he added that these helping, or auxiliary, offices issued forth from the pastoral office "as from the stem." It would not be wrong, therefore, to say of them, in view of their deriving from the one divinely instituted office, that they cohere in that office, since the duties performed are in each case and in the first place incumbent upon the pastoral office.[19]

A DCE who finds herself struggling to execute the vision for youth ministry as cast by the pastor may discover after much reflection and discussion that they are at philosophical odds. In that situation, the DCE is not in the right to assert that her training in youth ministry supersedes the pastor's vision. The DCE may attempt to win over the pastor and persuade him on the basis of that training that her vision is better suited for the congregation, but the final judgment is not the DCE's to make. Yet all of this does not negate the ministry of the DCE. Her work and vision are not of less value to the church. At times, they may be of far greater value. For example, the DCE may be in the best position to note the changing impact that culture is having on the understanding youth bring with them as they begin confirmation instruction, and thus may be better suited to envision necessary changes to the pedagogical approach taken during

---

18 Walther, *The Church and the Office of the Ministry*, 286.

19 Klug, *Church and Ministry*, 268.

confirmation. However, as much as there has been a justified tendency to avoid the establishment of a hierarchy in the Lutheran understanding of ministry, there are lines of authority and a distinction between those who have less authority and those who have more. Thus in the example above, the DCE might be in the right position to see and envision the necessary changes, but not in the right position to seek to enact those changes without pastoral support.

OTHER VOICES AT THE TIME OF WALTHER

In order to better understand Walther's conception of the Office of the Public Ministry, it may be beneficial to examine his work in context with other voices with whom he interacted and debated. Klug suggests the following:

> The studied, deliberate purpose of Walther is merely to emphasize that this office is the one divinely instituted office given to the church. Walther immediately adds, however, to this thesis that there may indeed be other offices in the church, but these flow from the one divinely ordained office as auxiliary, or derivative, since they carry out functions that belong fundamentally to the God-ordained pastoral office.[20]

Classically Lutheran, Walther holds in tension the singularity of the one office, while at the same time asserting the potential for the establishment of auxiliary offices which derive from that one office. In so doing, Walther stakes a claim on a middle position with regard to the understanding of the nature of the Office of the Public Ministry as it developed in the practice of the Lutheran church bodies forming around the time of the formation of the LCMS.

> According to Nafzger (LE, 139-142), Walther is an example of the "mediating school" on the doctrine of the ministry between an "episcopal school" which holds that the person who holds the ministerial office is the personal representative of Christ on earth and the "functional school" which holds that the office of the ministry is a human arrangement which functions to preach the Gospel and administer the sacraments. Rev. William Loehe and Rev. J.A.A. Grabau are cited as examples of the episcopal school while August C. Stellhorn and Rev. Dr. Arnold C. Mueller are associated with the functional school.[21]

While Stellhorn and Mueller will be addressed later, it is helpful to understand the disagreement between Walther and Löhe. Initially, Löhe was a great support of Walther and the new Missouri Synod, sending pastors and providing funding and support for the founding of a training school in Fort Wayne. However, the insistence of Walther on the locus of ministerial authority being in the congregation eventually became too much for Löhe.

---

20 Klug, *Church and Ministry,* 274

21 Toepper, "Is the Lutheran Teacher a Minister: Part I," 67.

Löhe held that the authority of the ministry was held by the ordained and not the congregation. Löhe was concerned that too much power was being placed in the hands of the local congregation in the theology of Walther. As a result, Löhe eventually severed his ties to the LCMS and began instead supporting the Buffalo Synod, sending pastors to support that church body as he has previously done for the LCMS. With Grabau, founder of the Buffalo Synod, Löhe found an understanding of the authority of the ministry more in line with his own. Nafzger credits Walther with seeking a compromise position in the dispute that arose with the Buffalo Synod.[22]

Nafzger also points out that, "In opposition to Carl Vehse, who wanted to reduce the office of the ministry to a mere public service enjoined to a person, Walther decisively held to the distinction of the 'office of the ministry' from the Priesthood of All Believers."[23] Walther was attempting to strike a balance. Nafzger argues that Walther's first three theses on *Church and Ministry* are offered against the functionalist position, while "theses 4, 9, and 10 reject certain aspects of the doctrine of the ministry held by the 'episcopal school.'"[24]

Walther and Löhe took up positions on opposing ends of the spectrum. Walther's emphasis was on the congregation, while Löhe's emphasis rested upon the Office of the Public Ministry. Johnson explains:

> Walther taught that the ministry grew out of the priesthood of believers with the congregation possessing the authority of the Amt. For sake of good order the congregation simply transfers it to one of its members. Therefore, the congregation is the bearer of the Keys and transfers (übertragen) such authority to the pastor. The pastor exercises his office in the name of the congregation.[25]

Citing Löhe's own writings, Johnson goes on to point out that Löhe held that by placing the authority of the keys in the hands of the congregation a half-measure is formulated. The concern Löhe had was how the authority to bind and loose sins can be held by a man who himself might lose the very authority to do so. Thus,

> Löhe held that the office of the ministry is a divine institution in its own right and does not derive its right and authority from the local congregation. Therefore, according to Löhe, the congregation does not transfer its powers to the pastor, but the pastor who fills the office is the instrument of Christ.[26]

---

22 Nafzger, "The CTCR's Report on 'The Ministry,'" 141.

23 Nafzger, "The CTCR's Report on 'The Ministry,'" 141.

24 Nafzger, "The CTCR's Report on 'The Ministry,'"142.

25 Johnson, "The Ministry and the Schoolmaster," 14.

26 Johnson, "The Ministry and the Schoolmaster," 14.

Citing Schaaf, Johnson notes that the shape of the dispute was formed around differing understandings of the origin of the *Amt* (office of ministry). "Both Grabau and Walther were agreed that the ministry was a divine institution and not a human invention, but they differed sharply in regard to the manner in which the authority of the ministerial office was given to the individual bearer of the *Amt*."[27] Grabau located the source of authority in the *Amt* while Walther placed that authority in the *Kirche*.

> So who is correct and who is in error? Sasse reminds us that the answer is both and neither. Either position can easily be defended in the Confessions and Holy Scriptures. The common danger of both positions, however, is for one, the congregation or the ministry, to be overemphasized at the expense of the other. When Walther overemphasizes the authority of the congregation, he risks ignoring the unique gift Christ has given in the office of the ministry. When Löhe overemphasizes the ministry, he risks removing from the priesthood such gifts as "emergency baptism" and "emergency absolution."[28]

In the end, this difference has the consequence of muddling the distinction between "the office of the ministry and the royal priesthood."[29] Further, when you factor in the service of commissioned ministers, this lack of clarity has resulted in a false dichotomy in which the commissioned minister has no clear home, being neither clergy nor laity.

CONCLUSION

In Walther, the LCMS had a mediating voice who was able to articulate a conceptualization of the Office of the Public Ministry that held to both a high view of the pastoral office, as well as a high view of auxiliary offices that branched from the pastoral office. While Walther is seen by some as having gone too far in a congregational direction, he managed to strike a balance that both upheld the Office of the Public Ministry alongside the role of the local congregation to call individuals into service in that office. Further, Walther held the Lutheran teacher in high esteem, while not having to resort to any loss of a high view of the Office of the Pastor. Unfortunately there have been too many occasions that we, as heirs of Walther's work, have struggled to maintain that necessary balance and have either denigrated the ministry of auxiliary workers or argued contrary to the clear teachings of Scripture and the Lutheran Confessions as it relates to the unique and singular nature of the Office of the Public Ministry. Thus the history of the LCMS has seen not only a lack of clarity on the position of auxiliary or commissioned workers, but has at times

---

27 Johnson, "The Ministry and the Schoolmaster," 15.

28 Johnson, "The Ministry and the Schoolmaster," 15.

29 Johnson, "The Ministry and the Schoolmaster," 18.

put them forward as what might be seen merely as a segment of the laity with no true ministerial function, or as bearers of and additional office beside the pastoral office. Future chapters will attempt to navigate through these competing positions, seeking to restore a properly Waltherian mediating position.

CHAPTER 5

The Diaconate

How does the diaconate relate to the discussion of commissioned ministry in the LCMS today? Upcoming in chapter 8, the origin of the diaconate and its implications for current church practice will be discussed. In this chapter, however, the diaconate will be discussed, in brief, as it was used in the ancient and medieval church.

In the diaconate of the ancient and medieval church, Ziegler notes that

> It is obvious that people introduced very many such offices that we call "ecclesiastical" for the sake of practical suitability. If they do not use them well, then we can rebuke such people because we nevertheless distinguish them correctly from other essential offices. Because these latter are necessary to the Church and because God Himself instituted them, they differ much from the practical ones and those that people invented for the convenience and support of the essential ones. Just as otherwise those that are judged on the basis of their usefulness are greatly inferior to those that are necessary; so also the ecclesiastical offices what is superior supports its essential office.[1]

There is a clear and proper distinction being made between those offices of a more practical nature and those instituted by God. These offices of the diaconate were instituted by the church in order to support the work of the essential office of the pastor. Those who bear these diaconal offices are not to exercise their ministry in a manner that detracts from the ministry of the pastor.

These diaconal offices have their origin in the determination of the church rather than having been instituted by Christ, as the pastoral office was. Due to this distinction, it is proper to note that "it is surely within the judgement of the Church to increase or decrease some according to certain circumstances, or even to remove them completely, as the thinking of the church demands."[2] This leaves those called into these ministries in a somewhat precarious position. Just as circumstances may call for the creation of new offices to serve the church, subsequent changes may render these offices no longer necessary, both on a congregational and national level.

Since the purpose of said offices is to support the ministry of the pastoral office, they derive their purpose accordingly. Ziegler notes that

---

1 Ziegler, *The Diaconate of the Ancient and Medieval Church,* 14.

2 Ziegler, *The Diaconate,* 20.

> After all, if the care of the poor and of the treasury of the church is entrusted to a deacon, what hinders this from being a temporary function of such a person because the duties that concern the treasury are commanded to be temporary and moveable by some shapers of the state? But if deacons be set up in such a way that they offer helpful work to elders in their ministry of the Word and sacraments, they shall claim more correctly that this duty is unending, namely, so long as they show themselves worthy of their calling.[3]

Thus the church, having instituted diaconal-type offices, ought to respect the ministry done by those serving in these offices and not eliminate them without great reflection and without due consideration of the implications for the church and those serving the church.

While there is cause to distinguish the nature of diaconal ministry from that of the pastor, the first deacons were ordained for their own ministry on behalf of the church.[4] But what are we to make of the reports of Scripture that might lead one to believe that these first deacons exercised ministry that we more properly associate with the pastoral office? Ziegler points out that

> Furthermore, one perhaps cannot deny that, although the first deacons remained in this ministry of theirs for a long time, with the passage of time they were placed in charge of other duties in the Church and especially of delivering homilies to the people. . . . Those who ministered scrupulously in a lower order and have given good proof of their skillful involvement will be promoted to a higher and superior rank, becoming worthy of the priesthood of the presbytery of the Church. . . . Others, then, would be sufficient to take care of the ministry of sustenance, or, if the deacons could survive that extra labor, they could still retain the office of the diaconate and of the presbytery.[5]

From this, it would seem that the early church may have assessed the needs of the local fellowship as well as the talents and character of the individual deacon in order to determine a course of action, rather than having a blanket policy. That said, however, this does not justify any sense of arbitrariness on the part of church leadership. As critical temporary needs may have arisen, the early church may well have allowed for deacons to serve in a role more suited for a pastor or apostle. "Let us grant, however, that from the beginning the apostles intended a ministry of deacons that at some time could be exchanged with the ministry of the Word or connected therewith. Yet as I have said, this

---

3 Ziegler, *The Diaconate*, 131.

4 Ziegler, *The Diaconate*, 44.

5 Ziegler, *The Diaconate*, 54.

was not their first ministry."[6] However, for those who demonstrate the aptitude and calling, it would have been far more appropriate to ordain the deacon as a pastor rather than merely entrust pastoral duties to a deacon. In this way, the early church kept order while remaining responsive to needs.

Despite the references to the diaconate being a lesser office or being distinguished from those that are essential, Ziegler still offers an affirmation from history of the ministerial importance of these diaconal offices. Deacons are listed along with elders and "the rest of the ministers of the church" as "a sort of sacred group and specific order" arguing that "anyone promoted into these sacred orders is said to be ordained."[7] They further note that "(a)n ordination of this kind is a confirmation of legitimate calling through which the ministry of the Church is commended to a called or suitable person for the performance of this duty."[8]

In light of the prior discussion on the lack of the vote for commissioned ministers in the LCMS, it is intriguing to find a discussion of the suffrage of deacons in the Ziegler text.

> Diaconal suffrage indeed was standard practice in the Church for some time. Later, however, the bishops became discontented with the power that they held by divine right and set neither a limit nor an end on their ambition. . . . The mouth of the deacons was stopped up in councils and their voice was cut off. In fact, lest there be anyone to try any such thing, the bishops no longer conferred the office of the diaconate to the learned but to the patently ignorant and to those barely trained.[9]

Where deacons had initially had a voice by vote in councils as the laity did, over time this voice was lost. The increasing practice of not ordaining the best and brightest into the diaconate would naturally have a negative impact on the respect given to those serving in that office. There would be a natural correlation between decline in the skill and education of deacons and the respect and leadership afforded to them.

This sets up an unfortunate and unnecessarily adversarial relationship between the pastoral office and the diaconate.

> The bishops have acted in the same way with their own deacons. The deacons very often turned their horns against their bishops, and the latter had to be afraid that the deacons ultimately wanted to know more than their bishops and that their authority as bishops would cease and perish

---

6 Ziegler, *The Diaconate,* 58.

7 Ziegler, *The Diaconate,* 115.

8 Ziegler, *The Diaconate,* 121–22.

9 Ziegler, *The Diaconate,* 225.

> completely. The bishops thought from the contrary point of view that they had to deny the deacons even the least thing that could ignite the tinder and provide occasion for attacking again the bishops' authority.[10]

The team that was to support each other's ministry fell prey to petty jealousies early in the history of the church. The trust necessary to serve together and the respect for one another's offices that, when lacking, often causes conflict today, is nothing truly new.

The balance between the distinctions of offices and the commonality of ministry together has been a struggle for centuries. Ziegler points out that

> Indeed, there may be a certain order and distinction among ministers of the Church according to the limits of the object in which they are engaged and according to the greater or lesser public usefulness of such to the preservation of the mystic body (i.e., the Church). Again, it may well be that one cannot engage and be involved in those different objects equally. Nevertheless, it is necessary that all occur on that ultimate goal, which is spiritual salvation.[11]

As with other aspects of Lutheran theology, a tension must be maintained in order to do proper justice both to the distinctions between offices and to their joint mission to reach the lost with the Gospel of Christ.

---

10 Ziegler, *The Diaconate,* 251.

11 Ziegler, *The Diaconate,* 255.

CHAPTER 6

Early LCMS History

WISCONSIN

An examination of the context of the LCMS's formative years will reveal a fuller picture of the relationship between the Office of the Public Ministry and commissioned ministry. One such element of that context can be seen in the theology of the Wisconsin Synod (WELS). Also a conservative, confessional church body, the history of the development of the WELS doctrine of ministry sheds light on the LCMS doctrinal development, both in where positions align and where they diverge.

While Walther articulates a high place for the Lutheran teacher, the LCMS he helped to found failed to arrive at a truly solid and satisfactory understanding of the place of the commissioned minister in congregational, district, and synodical life. From the start, there has remained an element of unresolved tension. This unresolved tension persists today. Just like a pastor, commissioned workers are synodically trained and called into ministry in local churches and schools. Commissioned workers serve on synodical and district boards and commissions, yet they remain disenfranchised when district and synod meet in convention.

> There is historical precedent within the Missouri Synod for its position that the teaching ministry is an auxiliary ministry. The precedent began with Walther in 1851, was supported by many examples after that, and became institutionalized by the CTCR report on "The Ministry: Offices, Procedures, and Nomenclature" in 1981.[1]

Yet, inasmuch as the role of the Lutheran teacher has a strong history in the LCMS, the understanding of just what it means to be an auxiliary ministry has been less than clear throughout the history of the LCMS.

While the LCMS position on the pastor's role in the local congregation remained stable during its early history, according to Wohlrabe, there was not complete agreement on the place of auxiliary offices in the doctrine of the ministry. Some held that the Lutheran teacher had a divine call; others rejected this claim. Still others held that the Lutheran teacher had a dual call which was both secular and divine, for the Lutheran teacher's authority and call were considered by some to derive as much from the parents of the child as from the church. In that latter conceptualization, a sort of dual call again left the Luther-

---

1 Toepper, "Is the Lutheran Teacher a Minister: Part III," 265.

an teacher in unclear territory between the clergy and laity.[2]

Furthermore, from the perspective of the WELS there were concerns with Walther's identification of the Office of the Public Ministry with the pastoral office. WELS theologians began to interpret the one office of the ministry in the abstract, allowing for one office in the abstract and multiple offices in the concrete.[3] Peperkorn summarizes the Wauwatosa position (so named after the WELS Wauwatosa Seminary) as arguing that while the Scriptures instituted a Gospel ministry, no specific form for that ministry is prescribed. The concrete form of pastoral ministry could be argued to be one form of public ministry among others.[4] As will be seen later, this position eventually found its way into the LCMS in the mid-twentieth century.

Walther's use of *Predigtamt* and *Amt* has been at the center of much of this controversy. John Brug, a WELS theologian, argued that J. T. Mueller's translation *Predigtamt* as "pastoral office" falsely implies that the pastor not the congregation holds the office.[5] He sees this translation as obscuring other offices. He argues that Walther is less than clear in his usage of language in distinguishing between the pastoral office and other offices.[6] In Brug's estimation, positing the pastoral office as the only divine office of ministry leaves the Lutheran teacher wondering about the legitimacy of his or her own call. Implying in any way that the ministry of the Lutheran teacher is based on delegated authority gives the impression that the teacher's call is not really an office of ministry.[7] Peperkorn notes that the Wauwatosa understanding of Walther's *Amt* was of Gospel ministry taken in the abstract, which may be made concrete in a variety of forms.[8]

The LCMS has historically argued against reducing the Office of the Public Ministry to the abstract. For a reduction of the Office of the Public Ministry to an abstract idea allows functions to be separated from the office. Such a conclusion has been consistently rejected, despite the influence of this WELS-type approach, which will be discussed further later on.

BRANCH OFFICE

Since the time of Walther, auxiliary offices were often described as branching off of the pastoral office. "The preacher should therefore never forget that

---

2 Wohlrabe, "An Historical Analysis of the Doctrine of the Ministry in The Lutheran Church—Missouri Synod," 12.

3 Wohlrabe, "An Historical Analysis," 12–13.

4 Peperkorn, "C. F. W. Walther's Kirche und Amt and the Church Office Debate between the Missouri and Wisconsin Synods in the Early Twentieth Century," 309.

5 Brug, *The Ministry of the Word*, 403.

6 Brug, *The Ministry of the Word*, 404.

7 Brug, *The Ministry of the Word*, 405.

8 Peperkorn, "C. F. W. Walther's Kirche und Amt," 310.

the school teacher is also counted among the ministers of the Church, administers an auxiliary office branched off of his [the pastor's] office, and is likewise his colleague in this respect."[9] P. E. Kretzmann (1883–1965) concurs that auxiliary offices branch off from the pastoral office and are distinguished by the specific functions each auxiliary office is created for. Holding or bearing an auxiliary office conveys a divine call due to the office having its source in the pastoral office.[10]

In this discussion, a lack of proper distinction between ordained and commissioned ministers causes confusion. There are occasions where Walther suggests an equivalency between assistant pastors and teachers, and that lack of distinction potentially reduces pastoral ministry to functions and rightly would be seen as a low view of the pastoral office. Yet the ministry of the pastor is more than the execution of a set of tasks or functions. For the divine origin of the office establishes the pastoral office as more than those functions associated with it. A lack of distinction seems to be at work in the position of the Wauwatosa men; for they argued that the Office of the Public Ministry generally is seen in the abstract, while its functions take shape in the concrete form of various offices, including the pastoral office. Ministry does not exist absent the concrete expressions found in the local congregation or school, thus to discuss ministry in the abstract is to analyze concepts about ministry apart from the office bearers called to follow in the ministry of Christ. Ministry always has a context that involves both those who minister and those who are ministered to.

This lack of distinction manifested itself in another way. Wohlrabe points out that while Walther understood the Lutheran teacher to be a branch office of the pastorate, the Lutheran teacher was not given the right to vote in synodical conventions; and he was not considered a layman, because he was a holder of the Office of the Public Ministry, though not fully.[11] This was not, however, a view held by all during the formative years of the LCMS.

The relationship between the Lutheran teacher and pastor was addressed by Wilhelm Sihler (1801–85). Sihler emphasized that there ought to be an element of humility on the part of both the pastor and the teacher in their relationship with one another. While the pastor was to be in the supervisory role, the submission of the Lutheran teacher was not to be taken as forced subservience. There was to be a respect and brotherly love between teacher and pastor. They were to provide for one another a comfort and admonition.[12]

---

9 Walther, *Pastoral Theology*, 463.

10 Wohlrabe, "An Historical Analysis of the Doctrine of the Ministry in The Lutheran Church—Missouri Synod," 101.

11 Wohlrabe, "An Historical Analysis," 67–68.

12 Wohlrabe, "An Historical Analysis," 65.

A series of articles were published in *Der Lutheraner* by J. C. W. Lindemann (1827–79). In the first article, Lindemann put forward the notion of teachers as servants of the Word in their teaching in Lutheran schools. He further maintained that the teacher could be called upon to read a sermon or teach confirmation class, among other pastoral duties, during a pastoral absence.[13] It was made clear, however, that these were not the primary nor typical responsibilities of the Lutheran teacher.

In the next article, Lindemann articulated a position of the teacher as dual called. Similar to the view of E. A. W. Krauss (1851–1924) of the Addison Teachers Seminary (now Concordia University Chicago), the teacher was seen to have a secular vocation when teaching subjects that are not strictly theological in nature and as a branch office of the pastorate when teaching religiously oriented subject matter. Krauss held that the teacher who exclusively taught secular subjects was at liberty to exchange that vocation with any other secular vocation, in a way that the teacher of religious matters was expected not to do.[14]

This creates an unhelpful tension in the understanding of one's own call in the life of the Lutheran teacher. If the subjects taught by a given teacher were to change, would that of necessity impact their status? Should a high school teacher not accept a call to teach math?

A. J. Buenger published an article in an 1893 issue of *Evangelish–Lutherisches Schulblatt* (the official teachers journal of the day) in which he noted that a teacher is a parental representative and the teacher's office is a branch from the ministry of the pastor. He was, however, careful to make it clear that this did not mean that the teacher's office was to be equated with the pastoral office. Still, as an assistant of the pastor, the teacher was still to be understood as having a place within the public ministry.[15]

Speckhard, in a paper originally presented in 1897 to the North and West Michigan Conference of pastors and teachers, articulated the view that while the teacher was not a pastor, he was still a public servant of the Word. For Speckhard, the confusion related to the office of the teaching ministry and came from the Wauwatosa argument for ministry as *in abstracto*. He held that the office cannot be seen in the abstract because it cannot be said to exist within the congregation in any less than a concrete manner. There is no command for an office of teacher, yet Speckhard still held that the teacher had a divine call. This he established not on the teaching ministry being a concrete form of the abstract office of ministry, but rather as derived from the congregation creating the office in Christian liberty.[16]

---

13 Wohlrabe, "An Historical Analysis," 68.

14 Wohlrabe, "An Historical Analysis," 70.

15 Wohlrabe, "An Historical Analysis," 103.

16 Wohlrabe, "An Historical Analysis," 106.

In a similar vein, some held that the Priesthood of All Believers, gathered as the local church or a church body, is able to create special positions, like that of the teacher, as a branch or auxiliary office of the public ministry. In this manner, the teacher is set apart in his ministry from the pastor in a specific calling to teach God's Word to children. The teacher is therefore made a servant of the Word and partaker of the public ministry as called by the congregation.[17]

Zobel wrote in the *Lutheran School Journal* in 1921 a series of theses that sought to explain the divine nature of the call for the Lutheran teacher. Zobel argues in these theses that the teacher's office is divine because it is an office created by the church and entrusted with specific functions of the Office of the Public Ministry. Thus the teacher's office may be seen as divine just as its source in the pastoral office is divine.[18]

Note that, according to his third thesis, the church is under no obligation to call teachers. For that matter, the church is under no obligation to call or establish any of the auxiliary offices found in the LCMS today, nor any that the LCMS might deem necessary in the future. There is nothing requiring their establishment; likewise, the church is not obligated to maintain said office(s).

This applies both for the synod as a whole as well as for individual congregations. A church that has had a day school and elects to close the school due to financial difficulties, for example, no longer has need of called teachers. If a DCE takes a call to a new congregation, the church that DCE is leaving might wish to call a new DCE to continue that vital ministry, but they are at liberty to not call a new DCE as circumstances demand. However, the same does not hold for the calling of a pastor. The church is not at liberty to call a DCE rather than a pastor if they are financially able to afford only one called worker.

Thesis four outlines the rationale used in the establishment of an auxiliary office. There must be a need that the congregation or church body recognizes as necessitating greater attention than can be provided by the current office bearers. Specialized training for bearers of the newly established office may be necessary and might not be feasible to provide for those in other offices.

William C. Kohn (1865–1943), president of Concordia Teachers College, River Forest, maintained the divinity of the teachers call. Noting that God calls church workers mediately (i.e., through the call of the congregation), Kohn stressed that the call of the Lutheran teacher is the same as the call of the pastor. Both are God's servant whom He calls into their respective offices. The pastor is called to the entire Office of the Public Ministry, whereas the Lutheran teacher is called specifically to teach children about Jesus.[19]

---

17 Wohlrabe, "An Historical Analysis," 107.

18 Wohlrabe, "An Historical Analysis," 108–9.

19 Wohlrabe, "An Historical Analysis," 110.

L. August Heerboth published an article in the *Lutheran School Journal* in 1931, in which he puts forward what Wohlrabe sees as a seemingly representative view of the synod at the time on the matter. Heerboth held that the Lutheran teacher was the bearer of a truly divine office. He saw the office of the Lutheran teacher as a public ministry, in that it was done on behalf of others. Heerboth does distinguish the fact that while the pastor is called to care for the entire congregation, the teacher is called only to a certain part of that ministry. He was careful to make clear that the teacher is not a pastor, yet still maintained that the office is just as divine as that of the pastor.[20]

To be clear, saying that this was the majority position does not negate those who argued against the divinity of the teachers call. Wohlrabe does, however, point out that there was a lack of controversy on this matter at this point in the synod's history.[21] It would seem that during the early years of the synod, the disagreements related to the nature of the call of the teacher remained uncontentious enough to avoid open conflict. That would change just before the dawn of the twentieth century.

WOMEN AS LUTHERAN TEACHERS AND DEACONESSES

Women had been teaching for many years during the formative period of the LCMS. However, it was not until 1897 that the question of how women teachers fit within these arguments for the divinity of the teaching office were officially addressed. An article by George Stoeckhardt published in *Lehre und Wehre* stated that it was right for the church to have female teachers. Further, Stoeckhardt used the same line of argumentation that the church is able to establish new offices and thus an office open to women as Lutheran teachers was possible to be instituted in order to teach children.[22]

Though there were 252 women teaching in Lutheran schools by 1913, it was not until 1919 that women were able to enroll at one of the LCMS teachers colleges. While this provided for improved preparation for the women teaching in the LCMS, their work was not seen as equivalent to that of their male counterparts. John Eiselmeier wrote in the *Lutheran School Journal* of his concerns of the feminization of the teaching profession in 1925. Eiselmeier[23] was concerned that the presence of too many women teachers might have a feminizing effect on the boys, as they might lack enough male role models to emulate.[24]

---

20 Wohlrabe, "An Historical Analysis," 110–11.

21 Wohlrabe, "An Historical Analysis," 111.

22 Wohlrabe, "An Historical Analysis," 135.

23 Wohlrabe, "An Historical Analysis," 138.

24 The trend toward a large majority of female elementary and early childhood teachers may be contributing to what some are now calling a boy crisis (see Farrell and Gray, *The Boy Crisis*, 28-33). This in no way delegitimizes female teachers, but rather speaks to the need to encourage both young girls and boys to enter teaching at all levels.

While female teachers were able to be employed by synodical schools, it was not until 1973 that female teachers were included on the roster of synod.[25] During this time, female and male teachers served side by side, but were not similarly recognized. Only after 1973 were female teachers recognized officially and made callable by synod schools.

During this same time, deaconess ministry was making its way into the LCMS. Many of the founders of the LCMS were aware of the ministry of deaconesses from their prior time in Germany.[26] An article in *Der Lutheraner* from 1869 points out how the deaconess of the New Testament and the deaconess of the nineteenth century as promoted by Löhe and others were not by definition the same office.[27] This, however, was precisely the point that early advocates of the office of the deaconess were after. They saw a need to see the diaconate as an evolving response to the church's needs. The LCMS, however, was not quick to adopt the deaconess for its own ministry.

In his work to establish the deaconess in the LCMS, Fredrick W. Herzberger was careful to argue that the deaconess was an office separate from that of the public ministry. Advocating for the work of the deaconess, Herzberger argued that "Because of the fact that all other offices in the Church are but human ordinances. They can be and ought to be created as the exigency and the welfare of the local congregation demands. But they must all have their root in the divinely appointed Ministry and stand in vital relation to it."[28] Through his work, the pan-Lutheran Lutheran Deaconess Association was established in 1919.

Through both the addition of women to the ranks of Lutheran teaching and the establishment of deaconess ministry in the LCMS, women entered into the conversation on the role of auxiliary offices. As will be documented in the next chapter, this was only the beginning of change in how the church looked at these offices. Some of these were changes for the better, some were not.

---

25 Suelflow, *Heritage in Motion*, 465–66.

26 Naumann, *In the Footsteps of Phoebe*, 3.

27 Naumann, *In the Footsteps of Phoebe*, 14.

28 Naumann, *In the Footsteps of Phoebe*, 23.

CHAPTER 7

Twentieth-Century Development

Introduction

An examination of the relationship between the Lutheran teacher and those auxiliary offices established during the twentieth century[1] suggests at least two areas worth discussion. One of these developments deals with legal challenges that the LCMS engaged in on behalf of its teachers. The other deals with some defenders of the office of the Lutheran teacher and the approach that they took in the justification of the Lutheran teacher as an office of the church. Each theme provides context for the current understanding of auxiliary offices. Both bring with them baggage that needs unpacking in order to clarify an understanding of auxiliary offices moving forward as a church body in the LCMS. Both involve the functional view of the office of the ministry, counter to the traditional understanding of the office within Lutheranism.

THE EGGEN CASE[2]

In September of 1949, Eldor Eggen,[3] a teacher serving at St. Lorenz Lutheran School in Frankenmuth, Michigan, was the subject of spot check related to the filing of his taxes with the Internal Revenue Service.[4] At issue was whether as a teacher he was required to pay tax on the rental value of the house provided to him by the congregation. While it was clear with the IRS with regard to the qualification for pastors to do so for a parsonage, a similar claim on behalf of a teacher for a teacherage was challenged as outside the stipulations of the law, and thus Mr. Eggen was to report the rental value as taxable income.

In a brief on the case provided to F. A. Hertwig and S. J. Roth on the matter by P. M. Bretscher, A. C. Stellhorn, and A. C. Mueller, the claim was made that

> According to the teachings of the Lutheran Church—Missouri Synod, there is but one office in the Church, commonly called the office of the

---

1 New commissioned offices include DCE, DCO, DFLM, DPM, and Lay Minister.

2 The following description follows Wohlrabe, pages 247–52.

3 For details on the Eggen Case in context and as it applies today, see the LCMS Congregational Treasurer's Manual, www.lcms.org/Document.fdoc?src=lcm&id=1110.

4 Then, as now, the IRS allows that ministers deduct a housing or rental allowance from their taxable income: www.irs.gov/faqs/interest-dividends-other-types-of-income/ministers-compensation-housing-allowance/ministers-compensation-housing-allowance.

> ministry. This one office, however, subdivides into various functions such as preaching, teaching, administration of the Sacraments, visitation of the sick, care of the young people, and the like.[5]

Wohlrabe offers his concerns related to the response strategy taken in this brief and the legal response of the synod.[6] While successful in defending the legitimate practice of considering Mr. Eggen as having an auxiliary office of the ministry, doing so using the terms of the legal system resulted in the confusion of the synod's position. While defending the LCMS theological position with legal terms to a government agency seems reasonable, doing so and offering an argument, even internally, as seen in the brief cited above, placed more emphasis on a legal definitions rather than a theological understanding of the status of the teacher.

The line of reasoning used argued in essence that a teacher should be considered a minister by the IRS just as a pastor because they fulfill similar functions in their service of the church. It was noted that the functions of their service were not identical, diverging on a number of points. However, the argument concluded that since there was enough overlap between the role of the pastor and that of the teacher, especially as it related to the teaching of the Gospel, that they should receive equivalent treatment.

Further, it was argued that both the teacher and the pastor did, under certain circumstances, assume one another's ministerial functions. There were pastors who taught in small rural schools. Also, there were situations in which the teacher was asked to assume pastoral functions, such as preaching in the absence of the pastor.

A further concern, pointed out by Wohlrabe, was the manner in which this functional view of ministry was put forward on behalf of the synod, but without official recognition of this as the synod's position in convention. The typical deliberation and theological reflection that the LCMS undertakes in convention, especially as it relates to matters of theological importance, did not take place.

Stellhorn went so far as to comment in a letter to Roth that

> Rev. Hertwig refrain from saying that the pastor has the whole local ministry in a congregation where a teacher has been called; because it militates against the idea that the teacher has a part of the ministry in such a case, and it only gives the government men another argument that the teacher is not a minister, but merely an assistant to the minister. He should also not speak of the teacher as being an assistant to the pastor, or the pas-

5 Bretscher, *The Office of the Teacher in The Lutheran Church—Missouri Synod,* 2.

6 Wohlrabe, "An Historical Analysis of the Doctrine of the Ministry in The Lutheran Church—Missouri Synod," 251–52.

tor's assistant, for the reason just stated. It is not in agreement with Rev. Hertwig's argumentation otherwise, and will give the government men a lever to upset your argument.[7]

While there might be a sense in which there is legal wisdom to this advice, the full understanding of how the LCMS articulated the relationship between the pastor and teacher and their offices was recommended to be muted for the expediency of winning a legal argument. The goal of winning the case dulled the general sense of understanding of the very ministry that was being defended.

None of this necessarily undermines the argument that auxiliary offices are branches of the pastoral office. However, this line of reasoning utilized an improper means to arrive at a proper goal, and furthermore, it introduced terminology that obscures rather than clarifies the issue, lending some to see the argumentation of this particular legal case as the central feature of the case for the ministry of commissioned workers. Though these offices lack the divine mandate of the pastoral office, "they participate in the public office of the ministry."[8] It remains valid to assert that "because a person serving in one of these auxiliary offices received a call through a congregation or a collection of congregations, the call to such an auxiliary office (is) considered divine."[9]

A. C. STELLHORN

August Conrad Stellhorn was the first secretary of schools for the LCMS, serving in that capacity from 1921–60. From this influential position, Stellhorn was able to provide what he believed to be a necessary argument on behalf of the call of teachers in the LCMS. Because some in the LCMS were concerned about the Lutheran teacher's role, Stellhorn was motivated to defend the divine nature of the call of the Lutheran teacher.

Stellhorn pointed out that the original method of education for pastors and teachers occurred at the same institutions. From this, he claimed that the synod did not originally differentiate between the two.[10] Despite this claim, he recognized and struggled with the reality that the Lutheran teacher, though a member of synod in the same way a pastor is, was from the beginning merely granted advisory status and no vote at district and synodical conventions.

According to Toepper, Stellhorn rejected the idea of auxiliary offices branching off from the pastoral office. Rather, he posited a conception of ministry in which the pastorate was not to be considered synonymous with the Of-

---

7 Stellhorn, *Letter to Supt. S. J. Roth, October 7, 1949*, 1.

8 Wohlrabe, "An Historical Analysis," 284.

9 Wohlrabe, "An Historical Analysis," 284–85.

10 Toepper, "Is the Lutheran Teacher a Minister: Part I," 65.

fice of the Public Ministry.[11] Stellhorn, as well as others like A. C. Mueller, held a view in which all offices, including the pastoral office, were branches from a general office of ministry.

Figure 10 demonstrates Stellhorn's and Mueller's teaching; they placed the pastoral office on an equivalent standing with all other offices in the church. Also, noteworthy is the functional understanding of this approach, which brought into the LCMS a view of ministry held by the WELS, and previously rejected by Missouri. The diagram listed as the incorrect view was in fact the traditional Missouri position.

FIGURE 10

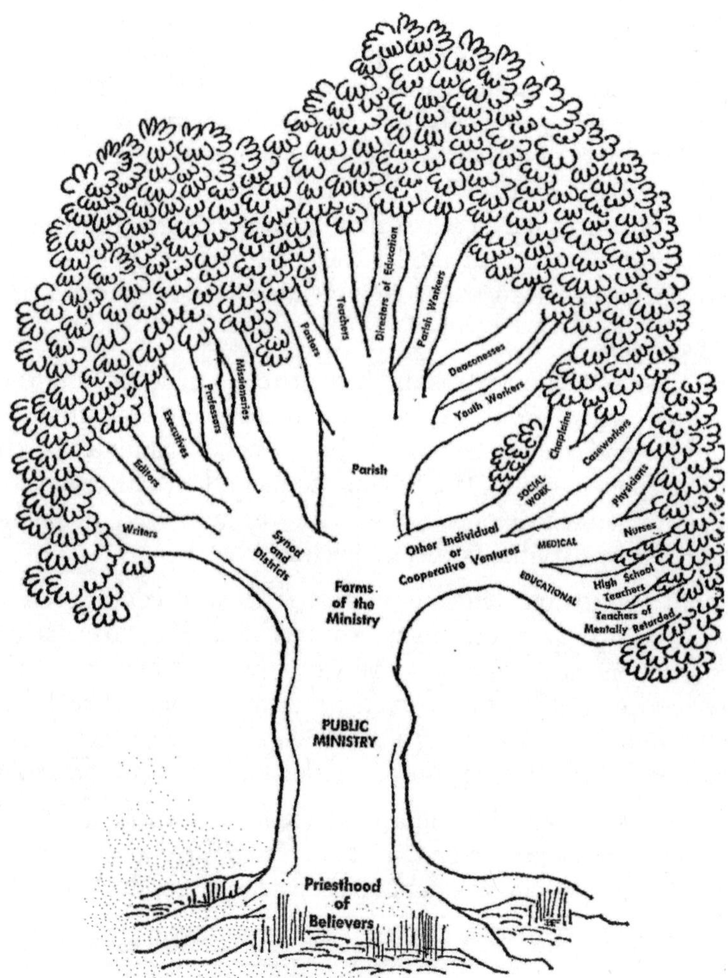

This diagram of Stellhorn and Mueller runs contrary to Walther and the official teachings of the LCMS.[12]

11 Toepper, "Is the Lutheran Teacher a Minister: Part II," 130.

12 Stellhorn, *Tree Diagram*, 1.

Of further note, from figure 10 one notices the listing of executives, editors, and professors along with pastors and teachers. While it might be taken for granted that a pastor who is called to serve as a professor or a teacher called to serve as a district education executive would still be considered called, this has not always been clearly understood as such.

In 1930, Alfred Kowert, a teacher in Milwaukee, was offered a position as the Superintendent of Schools for the Northern Wisconsin District.[13] His brother, Henry, wrote to Stellhorn out of his concern that the offer was not a call. In a letter to J. R. Harmening on the matter, Stellhorn argued that the superintendent should receive a call just as a professor is to receive a call.[14] This line of reasoning looked back in the history of the synod to Walther's argument for the divinity of the call for a professor as seen in his address at the installation of Prof. Adolph Biewend, as well as in his essay *Why Should Our Pastors, Teachers and Professors Subscribe Unconditionally to the Symbolical Writings of Our Church?* delivered at the Western District Convention in 1858.

The concern was how a call can be issued without a local congregation being the issuing body. How could a university, district, or synod itself issue a call? Stellhorn supported Kowert when he declined the offer on the grounds that the position was worthy of a call and that a district, just as a university and synod, is able to issue a divine call.

Reviewing a number of letters exchanged between Stellhorn and others demonstrates that in his position as Secretary of Schools, he was on the frontlines defending the divine nature of the call of teachers against those who were less than supportive of the call of the Lutheran teacher.

In a letter to A. W. Banke, Stellhorn pushed back on those "who held that a teacher had a twofold call – partly divine and partly civic."[15] Stellhorn further stated that

> You are quite right when you deplore the lack of a definite stand on the part of our leaders with regard to the divinity of the teacher's call. Everybody can practically say what he likes. Here is one case of a lack of unity of doctrine in our own midst. Those who put the teacher's call on the level with the monitor in Sunday school, or the deacon, have never impressed me as friends of the teachers, but rather as theological egotists; their intention is not to build, but to stand in the way of certain builders, or to put the hod-carrier on the same level with the brick-layer. I am sorely disgusted with such unfriendly destroyers under the guise of friendly advisers and teachers of the truth.[16]

---

13 Kowert, *Letter to A. C. Stellhorn dated November 29, 1930*, 1.

14 Stellhorn, *Letter to J. R. Harmening dated December 30, 1930*, 1.

15 Stellhorn, *Letter to A. W. Banke dated September 11, 1934*, 1.

16 Stellhorn, *Letter to H. Hillman dated October 5, 1934*, 4.

Stellhorn believed that too much patience had already been granted to those who sought to, in his view, destroy the schools of the LCMS. He saw these attacks on the call of the Lutheran teacher as part of a larger lack of support for the LCMS system of schools.

Stellhorn argued in *The Lutheran Teacher's Position in the Ministry of the Congregation* that "When the term 'ministry' is applied only to the pastorate, we use it in a highly restricted sense; for it embraces much more, and is properly applied also to the office or commission of the Church or the congregation."[17] Further, he suggests that "The 'one divinely instituted office,' that is, the general ministry of the Christian Church, requires many and various church positions, commonly called offices."[18] Stellhorn argued that Christ did not institute permanent church offices, an argument that runs directly counter to the traditional Lutheran understanding that the pastoral office was established by Christ and held initially by the apostles. He instead argues for a divinely instituted Office of the Public Ministry that is more generic, which provides the church Christian liberty to establish the pastoral office in its current form.[19]

Presenting at the Western District Teachers Conference in 1952 Stellhorn discussed both the private and public ministries of the Lutheran teacher:

> You teachers are both private and public ministers of God. Your private ministry is not necessarily something that you must perform only in a private place, such as the home, on in a conversation with a person; it simply means a service for which you have not special call from your fellow Christians. Thus, when you speak in a voter's meeting, or at a conference or convention, you are performing your private ministry, although you speak publicly. On the other hand, your public ministry is not necessarily something that is performed in a public place. Whether you teach in a secluded classroom or render musical service in public worship, you are preforming a public ministry because you have been chosen to render such services in behalf of all the members of your congregation. The term "public" means all the people, before all the people, or in behalf of all the people.[20]

If a teacher teaches her own children as students in the classroom, is she serving as a parent or a called teacher? In order to help Lutheran teachers to understand the nature of the calling, Stellhorn was attempting to help teachers distinguish between what they do in public ministry (i.e., the teaching of the children in the Lutheran school) and what they do in their private ministry

---

17 Stellhorn, *The Lutheran Teacher's Position in the Ministry of the Congregation*, 2.

18 Stellhorn, *The Lutheran Teacher's Position in the Ministry of the Congregation*, 3.

19 Stellhorn, *The Lutheran Teacher's Position in the Ministry of the Congregation*, 4.

20 Stellhorn, *The Lutheran Teacher in the Ministry of the Church*, 1–2.

(i.e., what they do as members of the local congregation). However, his examples are not as clear as they can be, confusing the very definition of what public ministry even means. Does a pastor step out of the Office of the Public Ministry and practice his role as a member of the Priesthood of All Believers when he speaks at a district convention, and then does he step back into the Office of the Public Ministry when he preaches? There are for certain very different purposes for the communication in each situation, but the call of the pastor remains the same. Returning to the example of a called teacher teaching her own children in the Lutheran school: we must distinguish between the private instruction, teaching the faith at home as a father or mother, and the public ministry, teaching the same content in the classroom.

Later in his presentation, Stellhorn argues that

> Whatever the offices established by a Christian congregation or the Christian Church in the name of the Lord, to carry out the divinely-instituted and permanent office of the Church, they are parts or branches of that one office of the Church, and therefore offices of God, instituted by the Lord through His Church.[21]

Here Stellhorn moves from the traditional understanding of the pastoral office as the permanent, divinely instituted office to a general office as he had argued elsewhere. He further comments that "The Bible knows nothing of auxiliary offices to some other office, though one office certainly is an aid to another office, or to all offices.[22]" True, the language of Scripture does not specifically use auxiliary office terminology, but as will be explored in the next chapter, the Bible does provide an example for how the church may establish offices to support and assist the pastoral office and the ministry of the pastor.

While in many cases Stellhorn drew support from the writings of Walther, he argues against Thesis VIII on *Kirche und Amt,* which stated that "The preaching office is the highest office in the Church, from which flow all other offices in the church."[23] Approaching ministry using a functional understanding as held in the WELS, he contended that

> The fact is, both offices have the highest function of the ministry, and both have also what Luther calls "lesser offices," such as baptizing, distributing Communion, leading the singing in public worship, directing the choir. The fact is further, all offices of the Church that have to do with the building and caring for the Church in the name of God, which is done only by means of applying the Word of God, have the highest function of the ministry.[24]

---

21 Stellhorn, *The Lutheran Teacher in the Ministry of the Church,* 11.

22 Stellhorn, *The Lutheran Teacher in the Ministry of the Church,* 11.

23 Walther, *The Church and the Office of the Ministry*, 284.

24 Stellhorn, *The Lutheran Teacher in the Ministry of the Church,* 12–13.

Though perhaps unintended by Stellhorn, this approach, while it uplifts the ministry of the Lutheran teacher, does damage to a high view of the pastoral office. If the pastoral office is merely an office in that it is a collection of functions of ministry, then could not the church realign such functions into another structure and eliminate the office of the pastor? This may not have been the goal of Stellhorn; however, his approach taken to its logical conclusion would leave more freedom than even he intended to grant.

Stellhorn attempts to place his argumentation in a form that appears rather modest when he states that

> In our efforts before the government to have the Lutheran teacher recognized and classified as a minister of the Gospel, we did not try to show that he is really a pastor, or a king of pastor. No, we took his office just as it is, and let him be a Lutheran teacher, but argued that all the earmarks of his office and call, his special training, and everything else that goes with his service and standing in the Church, proves him to be a minister of the Church, or a minister of the Gospel, although he is not called a pastor.[25]

However, as noted above, his argument does more than perhaps he even intended. When arguing that "In speaking of the highest 'office,' Luther and the Confessional Writings do not refer primarily to a church position, but to a ministerial function, or activity. Specifically they mean the preaching and teaching of the Word,"[26] it is hard to maintain that the argument is anything but a repudiation of the traditional position of the LCMS.

The failing of this position can be seen in Stellhorn's attempts to rebut Kretzmann's critique of his position. Kretzmann asserts that "1. The parish pastorate is an office, not merely a form or service or a position in the congregation based on historical development."[27] Stellhorn responds by asserting that

> Webster defines "office" as "that which a person does for, or with reference to, another or others; a service." So when the essayist says the parish pastorate is an office, we can fully agree: the occupant of the parish pastorate is the person who "does for … others," namely he does for the congregation the duties to which he has been called; in exactly the same manner in which a teacher does his duties to which he has been called by the same congregation. Webster further calls it a "service"; but the venerable essayist proceeds to say that the parish pastorate is "not … a service." How can a thing be two different things in the same breath?[28]

---

25 Stellhorn, *The Lutheran Teacher in the Ministry of the Church*, 15.

26 Stellhorn, *The Lutheran Teacher's Position in the Ministry of the Congregation*, 6.

27 Kretzmann, *Reviving a False Position with Regard to the Doctrine of the Call*, 4.

28 Stellhorn, *Comments Upon - Reviving a False Position with Regard to the Doctrine of the Call*, 3.

This is a return to a functional understanding of ministry, which the LCMS rejected and WELS adopted. In his response, Stellhorn attempted to head off Kretzmann's further conclusion, which would undermine the divine nature of the teacher's call. For Kretzmann continued

> 4. The ministry of the Word, in the wider sense, embraces all offices and forms of service which are inherent in the parish pastorate, but have been established by Christian congregations to assist the pastorate, whether in the form of the congregational or ecclesiastical offices (parish school teachers, deacons or elders, Sunday school teachers, deaconesses, chaplains, professors at church schools, etc.)
>
> 5. Yet we may never lose sight of the fact that the parish pastorate involves, directly or indirectly, the responsibility for <u>all souls</u> in the parish (1 Tim. 3–5; Acts 20:28; 1 Pet. 5:2).[29]

Rather than resorting to a functional view of ministry, Stellhorn may have been wiser to counter Kretzmann by pointing out that even in Kretzmann's language there is the seeds of an understanding of the place of the teaching office. Kretzmann's note that "all offices . . . are inherent in the parish pastorate" does not need to exclude the office of the teacher as a called office of the church. Stellhorn rightly counters that "there is only <u>one</u> office in the New Testament church."[30] In Kretzmann's own argument, he discusses that one office as having multiple office within. Stellhorn seems to have opted for a less defensible position in his efforts to defend the call of the Lutheran teacher.

In his seminal work *Schools of The Lutheran Church—Missouri Synod*, Stellhorn discusses the position of L. August Heerboth, which he considered to have closed the argument regarding the status of the Lutheran teacher.

> The office of the parish school teacher, as also the office of a professor at a church institution, is a branch of this ministry and therefore a divine office. However, there is a difference between the office of a pastor and that of a teacher: The pastor is called for the entire parish ministry, the teacher for a certain part of it. That part is outlined in the teacher's call, just as the duties of a professor and other church servants are outlined in their call, while the scope of the pastorate is already laid down in the Scriptures.[31]

Had Stellhorn remained closer in his explanation of this position in his own work, less confusion may have occurred.

---

29 Kretzmann, *Reviving a False Position with Regard to the Doctrine of the Call*, 4.

30 Stellhorn, *Comments Upon - Reviving a False Position with Regard to the Doctrine of the Call*, 5.

31 Stellhorn, *Schools of The Lutheran Church—Missouri Synod*, 462.

A. C. MUELLER

Arnold C. Mueller, who served on the Board for Parish Services, worked closely with Stellhorn and is most noted in the matter at hand as the author of *The Ministry of the Lutheran Teacher.* Like Stellhorn, Mueller expended a great deal of energy in defense of the ministry of the Lutheran teacher.

> Our church, recognizing the importance of early instruction in a Christian environment, has carried out the charge of the apostle, and trains men and women specifically for the vocation of teaching. Our teachers are engaged in the Christian training of the young; therefore they perform a part of the *ministerium ecclesiae,* or the ministry.[32]

For Mueller, what makes the Lutheran teacher a minister is their call to teach in a distinctively Christian environment. While non-called teachers fulfill their vocation in their teaching, inclusive of their work to witness to the love of Christ, the Lutheran school teacher, called to the service of the Lutheran church and school, has the further calling to establish this Christian environment in which the instruction of all subjects is to take place.

In a draft of a document, which would seem to have been a working document leading toward the eventual publication of *The Ministry of the Lutheran Teacher*, Mueller offers a helpful distinction.

> Because the men who are chiefly in our schools are called "teachers," people tend to think of them as being teachers, like teachers of our public schools, and not ministers of religion. Our fathers were careful to point out that our school teachers, with respect to their office, differ considerably from those who ordinarily are designated "teachers."[33]

For many today, this distinction remains hopelessly obscured. While there are reasonable, pragmatic reasons for a teacher to move between teaching in a Lutheran school or another Christian school or a public school, to eliminate the distinctions between those circumstances is problematic. Mueller points out that

> With respect to their office, the teachers employed by Christian congregation, differ from teachers employed in the public and in private schools, in that their office, according to its primary functions, is an office of the Church, and that they are servants of the Church because they teach God's Word publicly.[34]

Lost on many today is a sense in which the role of the Lutheran teacher is

---

32 Mueller, *The Ministry of the Lutheran Teacher*, 106.

33 Mueller, *Untitled partial document*, 7.

34 Mueller, *Untitled partial document*, 7.

substantively different than their public school counterparts. Perhaps there is a belief that the Lutheran teacher is expected to be theologically knowledgeable enough to teach the faith as a subject in their classroom, or perhaps even teach all subjects through a lens of faith, but on the whole that concept of the Lutheran teacher as office bearer is all too often obscured.

Further compounding this issue is the practice of contracting teachers rather than calling them. In some cases, teachers who are on synodical roster and could be called are not, and are merely contracted. In other cases, teachers who are not on the roster of the synod are hired, some who may be Christian but are certainly not Lutheran. While there are very good, pragmatic reasons that this takes place, the net effect on the Lutheran identity of the school may be the potential re-shaping of the school as a private school with some Christian foundation, rather than a distinctly Lutheran institution.

Holding our teachers to a higher standard would not only elevate their status within the congregation, but would elevate their own view of the work they are called to do. Citing Lindemann from *Schul-Praxis* from 1888, Mueller states that

> The election and call of the teacher is the responsibility of the entire congregation, and it is always a call for life (permanent as opposed to contract or a restricted period of service); for insofar as he is a servant of the Word, the Holy Spirit called him through the representatives of all the children of God in the congregation ... all members of the congregation obligate themselves to provide for the teacher's maintenance, so that he may always attend to the duties of his office and so that the school may fulfill its purpose.[35]

This high view of the call of the teacher as expressed by Mueller is something that many of our congregations would do well to emulate. While we will see shortly that his understanding of the teacher's call is problematic on other points, here he offers an encouragement for the congregation to engage directly in the calling of their teachers as well as their ongoing support. Too often the calling of teachers, for pragmatic reasons, is delegated to a school board. This however, disconnects the larger congregation from the ministry of the school and the teachers who serve in their name.

To understand how Mueller arrives at his view of ministry, it is worth examining his paper *The Status of the Parochial School Teacher.* The questions that Mueller sought to address in this paper included these:

> Does the office of school teacher exist in its own right, or is it an off-shoot of the pastorate? Is the office of the pastor coextensive with the "Ministerium Ecclesiae" (ministry of the church), or is the latter something

---

35 Mueller, *Untitled partial document*, 7.

general of which both the pastorate and the office of the teacher are branches? Is the pastorate the one divinely instituted office, and is the office of the teacher therefore merely an auxiliary office, and hence, not instituted by God?[36]

The concern was that if it could not be demonstrated that the teacher's office was instituted by God, that by extension it would be questionable whether that office was indeed divine or even to be considered a ministry of the church.

Mueller attempts to answer these questions, at one point citing Gerhard.

> Gerhard points out that the terms we have just studied are abstract terms, designating the office. He then proceeds to the concrete terms, which designate the incumbents of the office. He says some of these concrete terms apply to all ministers or servants of the Church, others only to certain classes of ministers or servants.[37]

As noted previously, this understanding of the office in the abstract and the functions of the offices of the church as the concrete expressions of that office was the view held by the WELS understanding of Walther. This was not the view of Walther as held within the LCMS, however, making its reintroduction by Mueller and others problematic.

Like Stellhorn, Mueller argued that the New Testament makes no reference to the concept of auxiliary offices. He states that "I am ready to accept the term 'auxiliary' for church functions which are an aid to the pastor but do not require proficiency in teaching the Word, but I refuse to apply this term to any servants of the Church who teach the Word, because the very concept is unscriptural."[38] Following this statement, Mueller seems to argue his point from Ephesians 4:12, though he likely had verse 11 in mind as well. The trouble is that if he intends to claim that this listing implies a set of various offices in the church, he is on less than firm footing.

Mueller goes on to say that instead of Scripture placing the entire public ministry upon a single man that Scripture instead "speaks of various offices of the public ministry, and does not subordinate one to the other."[39] Further, he suggests that "the position or office or the teacher, as it has developed, not by any specific precept of Scripture, but by the needs of performing the public ministry and in Christian liberty."[40] If Mueller, here, intends to connect the conception of the Lutheran teacher of modern day with the teacher mentioned

---

36 Mueller, *The Status of the Parochial School Teacher*, 1.

37 Mueller, *The Status of the Parochial School Teacher*, 3.

38 Mueller, *The Status of the Parochial School Teacher*, 4.

39 Mueller, *The Status of the Parochial School Teacher*, 4.

40 Mueller, *The Status of the Parochial School Teacher*, 5.

in Ephesians 4:11, he is making a move that cannot be sustained. It is clear from the context of the text that Paul does not have anything in mind remotely similar to the modern teacher. One ought to think more of the teaching aspect of the pastoral office rather than a school teacher to understand what Paul is getting at.

Later in the paper, Mueller argues that

> The pastor should maintain the dignity of the teacher's office, and the teacher should respect the man who is his pastor. Every loyal-hearted teacher recognizes the difference between the office of pastor and that of teacher. The teacher knows what his field of activity is. He does not try to arrogate to himself the office of the pastor.[41]

This is great advice regardless of what approach to understanding the office of ministry you might take. There ought to be a high view of all the work of our synod's church workers, something unfortunately not always practiced. It is truly necessary to recognize the differences between each office, especially the pastoral office as compared to all the commissioned offices. Through this recognition and understanding should flow a respect for the work done and the joint labor accomplished for the Kingdom.

In *The Office of the Ministry and the Lutheran School Teacher*, Mueller maintains that:

> If some are still puzzled because of Luther's statement that all offices are granted to the person who has the office of the Word delegated to him, let them bear the context in mind in which Luther is speaking. Luther maintains that one who has the authority to teach the Word does not need an additional priestly consecration in order to perform other ecclesiastical functions. We conceive of the pastorate as embracing functions like the following: preaching, teaching, administration of the Sacraments, visitation of the sick, etc. Luther's office of preaching is not identical with the pastorate as we conceive it, for he deliberately excludes the administration of Baptism. Certainly the call to preach the Gospel includes the power to exercise all the other functions of the ministry. But this does not mean that the pastor de facto exercises all the functions of the ministry, and that the office of teaching school or the function of preparing young men as pastors or teachers derives from the pastorate.[42]

Here Mueller seems to be attempting to argue that modern readers are mistaken to conclude that Luther only refers to the pastoral office in his writings. He justifies this claim by pointing to the context in which Luther was

---

41 Mueller, *The Status of the Parochial School Teacher*, 24.

42 Mueller, *The Office of the Ministry and the Lutheran School Teacher*, 29.

writing, stating that the office as used by Luther is not properly equivalent to the pastoral office as we have it today. However, rather than opening up room for an understanding of the teaching ministry as a distinct office, Mueller takes his argument a step too far, claiming that the teaching office is something unrelated to the pastorate. Like Stellhorn and the WELS functional view, Mueller is attempting to ground the teaching as well as pastoral ministry as two of many offices flowing from a larger Office of the Public Ministry.

A few pages later, Mueller offers support for pastors having the highest office, but in such a way that they are not synonymous with the Office of the Public Ministry. He claims that, "In so far as any Christian shares in the functions of teaching the Word, he has the highest office, whether pastor, teacher, or whatever his work may be."[43] Again, the influence of a functional understanding of the ministry is evident.

Stemming from this functional understanding, Mueller offers a discussion of Walther's use of *Predigtamt* and *Pfarramt* in his book *The Ministry of the Lutheran Teacher*. For Mueller, it would be a mistake to argue that these are equivalent terms. Mueller argues that the use of *Predigtamt* (preaching office) can be seen in a broad sense, encompassing all those offices that relate to the teaching of the Word. Mueller does not see *Pfarramt* (pastoral office) identical to the preaching office. Seeing the preaching office more broadly, Mueller is arguing for the divinity of the call for professors, teachers, editors, and others. Without this distinction, he concludes that these are merely man-made and without a divine call.[44] In this functional model, the pastor is but one office or form of many that combine to make the Office of the Public Ministry.

---

43 Mueller, *The Office of the Ministry and the Lutheran School Teacher*, 31.

44 Mueller, *The Ministry of the Lutheran Teacher*, 90.

FIGURE 11

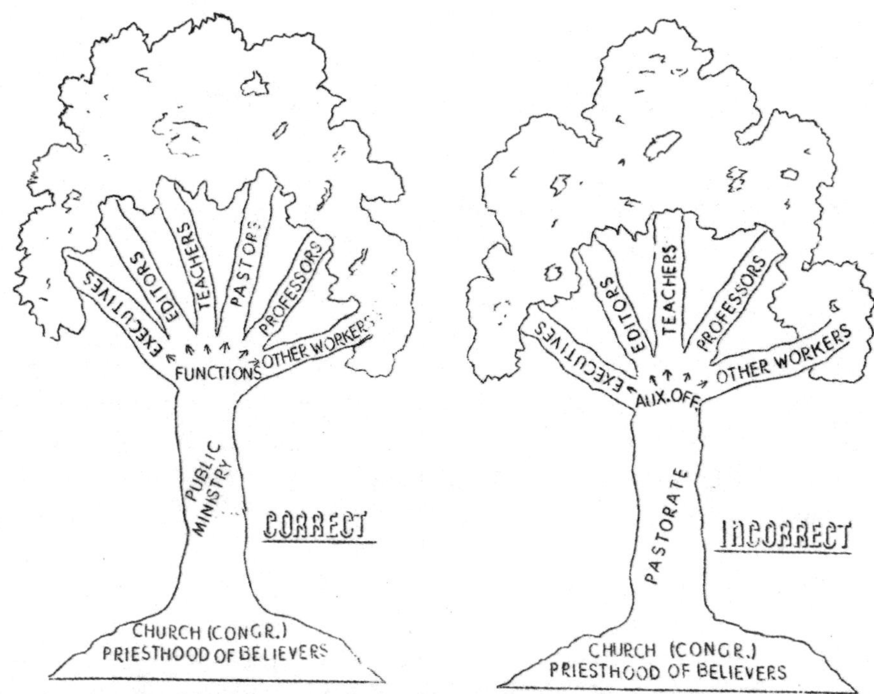

Mueller, *The Ministry of the Lutheran Teacher*, p. 10.

Mueller later argues that the translation of *Hilfsamt* as auxiliary office has been "unfortunate" in that it has allowed some to argue that only the pastorate is the "one divinely-instituted office."[45] In this argument, Mueller is correct to question the translation. As is noted in the more resent translation, a better rendering might be "helping office" rather than auxiliary.[46] However, this does not mean that the pastoral office is therefore not the "one divinely-instituted office." Arguing for the place of these offices—whether called "commissioned," "auxiliary," or "helping"—does not need to be done by claiming an equivalency of these offices with the pastoral office.

In the midst of this line of argumentation, Mueller offers a helpful note that has much bearing on the current discussion of the theology of commissioned ministers.

> The term "ministry" today suggests the pastor's office to most people. The church should have kept the original meaning of diakonia in mind. As we have seen, it is Paul's expression for all types of service rendered for the promotion of the Gospel. We may, therefore, speak of the teacher's

45 Mueller, *The Ministry of the Lutheran Teacher*, 93.

46 Walther, *The Church and the Office of the Ministry*, 286.

position as the "ministry of teaching" just as we may speak of the pastor's position as "ministry of preaching," for both are ministers in the sense in which Paul employs the word diakonia.[47]

Setting aside the recurrent issue of Mueller using terminology of this sort as a lever to equate the ministry of the pastor with the ministry of the Lutheran teacher, there is something worth considering. How do we understand διακονία? There is a tendency in the church toward being either overly loose with the term or conversely overly restrictive. How broad or narrow is appropriate, and is there a place for multiple uses of the term to suit the context under discussion?

S. A. SCHMIDT

Stephen A. Schmidt published *Powerless Pedagogues* in an attempt to examine the second-class treatment that many teachers in the LCMS were then and had historically experienced. Schmidt, like others already mentioned, wrestled with the lack of clarity related to the role or identity of the Lutheran teacher and by extension all those in commissioned offices.

Schmidt argued that the ministry of Lutheran teachers was subject to many professional limitations, which hampered their ministry. He comments that "Teachers were almost clergy, yet almost laymen."[48] He maintained that "This lack of clarity . . . was intentional for it tended to keep teachers in their places, auxiliary to the ordained clergy."[49]

Schmidt notes that the lack of a political voice within the structure of the LCMS can be seen as another way in which the voice of the Lutheran teacher is silenced. He comments that "The teaching ministers became advisory, neither lay nor clergy. They remained silent, their silence symbolized by lack of franchise. A few abortive attempts at political franchise were made. As these attempts failed, teachers retreated to their obedient station."[50] Schmidt's work sought to bring the needs and concerns of these educators back into the public discussion and receive the fair consideration, he believed, not present at that time.

Balancing between the clergy and laity in the structure and governance of the synod may have for the time created the compromise that Walther sought in order to establish the LCMS and allay the concerns of those still healing from the betrayal of Martin Stephan. But the long-term effect of the Lutheran teacher, who lacks franchise in this compromise, may not have been clearly foreseen. Schmidt makes the case that this lack of vote laid the foundation for

---

47 Mueller, *The Ministry of the Lutheran Teacher*, 92–93.

48 Schmidt, *Powerless Pedagogues*, 5.

49 Schmidt, *Powerless Pedagogues*, 5.

50 Schmidt, *Powerless Pedagogues*, 5.

much frustration for those in the teaching ministry.[51] While some would describe the balance as "nice," Schmidt sees simply expediency.

Compounding the lack of suffrage within the structures of the LCMS, the initial emphasis on the training of both pastors and teachers suffered an unfortunate change.

> It is clear from the evidence that teachers and pastors were to be trained together, in the same place and with the same curriculum. This the colonists (due to circumstances or philosophy) set a pattern for a new ministry in America—the ministry of teaching. One can make the case that the first seminary for church workers built by the Saxon Lutherans was originally intended to be a seminary for the training of teachers. That intention shifts as the needs of the immigrants called for more pastors. The intention, however, remained. The settlers were intent on educating a professional core of teachers and pastors. Unfortunately, as we shall see later, the training of teachers took second place and became relegated to a less dominant position in the church.[52]

Today, church work students may find themselves in the same classrooms studying for their respective roles, but this takes place at the undergraduate level. Only pastors and deaconesses are potentially classmates at the seminary level. Compounding the isolation, many seminarians matriculate outside the Concordia University System and may never come in contact with other church work students during their formation.

Due to this isolation, Schmidt contended that there developed a view on the part of the pastors of the LCMS that placed too much emphasis on their office.

> But this view was also nurtured at Concordia Seminary where clergymen often learned the unique specialty of their profession. Pastors graduated with a strong sense of pride in the profession of pastor and in their roles as spokesmen for God in the midst of His people. They spoke of "their" churches, "their" people, and "their" parishes.[53]

There is a great benefit to the formation of a pastor in such a manner that he recognizes that the ministry he is called into is a truly unique, noble, and in fact holy ministry. However, Schmidt's concern that this pride may result in a denigration of other offices that serve alongside the pastor remains a real concern for the church today.

---

51 Schmidt, *Powerless Pedagogues*, 20.

52 Schmidt, *Powerless Pedagogues*, 23.

53 Schmidt, *Powerless Pedagogues*, 30.

Lutheranism has long attempted to avoid the development of a rigid hierarchy. However, in a church structure such as a denomination some element of hierarchy is not only inevitable, one could argue that it is in fact scriptural. Headship ought not to be the issue. It is rather how this headship is fleshed out that Schmidt rightly voices concerns. When commissioned workers are treated as hired hands rather than called workers by their congregations and even their pastors, the way in which their call is understood is naturally impacted. There is a mutual solemnity that is enter into when a congregation or school calls a worker to serve in ministry in their midst. This solemnity places both a higher expectation on both the worker and the calling body. The worker is held to a higher standard to uphold the teachings of the Lutheran Confessions. The calling church or school is held to a higher standard to care for the worker as a minister, including the extent to which they will go to maintain their ministry in that place. Honoring all our called workers for their service is not merely something that ought to be done, but it encourages a quality of service far superior to the worker, who is seen as a hired hand. Insisting upon calling workers places service to Christ in the center of the exchange, binding the congregation or school together with the workers that they call.

Schmidt discussed the root of the tension between pastors and teachers in his doctoral dissertation.

> Early in Missouri's history the direct supervision of the educational agencies of the congregation was delegated to the pastor. He was superintendent of all parish educational efforts. That supervisory role was assumed on behalf of the congregation—authority by transfer. Such an arrangement was no doubt comfortable for the laymen; there was good German precedent for that arrangement. It was a practical solution for men busy working out a meager existence in a new land. The arrangement was no less comfortable for the pastor, particularly as teachers began to assist in the parish ministry. It assured the pastor of his dominant position and insured his position as head of the teacher. Needless to say the arrangement was the seedbed for discontent and teacher-pastor strife, as we shall note later.[54]

On the basis of Schmidt's argument, one is left with the impression that the headship of the pastor was more German than biblical. Further, one might be left to assume that this is a satisfactory approach as long as all parties are "comfortable" with the conditions of the arrangement. By this line of reasoning, discontent in the relationship between pastor and teacher is enough to call the entire structure into question. There is valid reason to work to overcome the discontent that may develop between pastors and teachers (and all commissioned workers for that matter), but this does not in any way justify the conclusion that pastoral oversight itself is the issue.

---

54 Schmidt, *Powerless Pedagogues*, 50–51.

Schmidt points out later in his dissertation that initially there was no evidence of "any large-scale dissention among teachers in the early days of the Missouri Synod."[55] He does say he believes that teachers were regardless "not in agreement with rigid congregational control" and that "The evidence also indicates that the position of teacher was sometimes a threat to the pastor."[56]

Schmidt returns to this threat in *Powerless Pedagogues* when he writes:

> Kretzmann was clear about his view of the good pedagogue. The Lutheran pastor or teacher was to be well indoctrinated in Lutheran Theology and Scripture and must agree that the Bible was the inspired, inerrant Word. His office was a noble one, "auxiliary" to the preaching ministry. One could almost refer to Kretzmann as an advocate of the teaching minister as a full participant in the total ministry of the parish. However, late in his service to Missouri, his fundamentalistic position was revealed. His response to an essay written by teacher, August C. Stellhorn, Superintendent of Lutheran Schools, regarding the ministry of the teacher, seemed almost defensively clerical. He appealed for clergy domination in the parish and made clear that the teaching ministry was not to be equated with the preaching ministry. The teaching ministry, he stated, was not central to the church's ministry but incidental, much as the office of Sunday school teacher, deacon, janitor, and organist. His reaction, we shall note later, was not unlike that of some other pastors when threatened by teachers over the issue of the paternalistic hierarchical polity of the church.[57]

What would have caused such acrimonious language to have crept into the debate? As has been seen, Stellhorn's effort to defend the call of the Lutheran teacher pushed too far in arguing for an equivalent understanding of the offices of pastor and teacher. Yet, Kretzmann's understanding of the teaching ministry as equivalent to "Sunday school teacher, deacon, janitor, and organist" seems equally excessive in the opposing direction.

Schmidt offers two competing images of what Lutheran teaching might be. On the negative side, he notes an all too real scenario where "The incessant reminders from the clergy that their office was 'lower,' 'less than,' 'under,' 'auxiliary to' the pastor's 'more holy office,' 'highest office,' could only undermine the professional dignity of the teacher."[58] No teacher can be expected to thrive in such circumstances. If the Lutheran teacher sees the elevation of the pastoral office as a slight to their own, they will quite naturally be impacted in the carrying out of the duties of their own office.

---

55 Schmidt, *Powerless Pedagogues*, 51.

56 Schmidt, *Powerless Pedagogues*, 51.

57 Schmidt, *Powerless Pedagogues*, 43.

58 Schmidt, *Powerless Pedagogues*, 61.

However, does the Lutheran teacher, of necessity, need to see the elevation of the pastoral office as an existential threat to their own ministry? No. The church insisting upon a high view of the pastoral office does not need to result in commissioned ministers feeling the need for a defensive posture. It is entirely appropriate to articulate, as this book is attempting to do, a high view of the pastoral office as well as a high view of commissioned ministry. The two are not mutually exclusive. Yet, as has been seen in this chapter, this time period in the LCMS was marked by some influential thinkers whose posture can hardly be seen as anything other than defensive.

CONCLUSION

This defensiveness did not serve commissioned ministry well. The work of A. C. Stellhorn, A. C. Mueller, Stephen Schmidt, and even more recently by Joel Lehenbauer has done much to bring a needed emphasis on the role of commissioned ministers in the ministry of the LCMS. Today the LCMS not only has Lutheran teachers, but to that list has been added DCEs, DCOs, deaconesses, DPMs, Lay Ministers, and DFLMs, greatly expanding the ministry of commissioned workers. However, structurally nothing has changed. Voting at conventions remains the purview of the clergy and the laity. Commissioned ministers still occupy an ill-defined middle ground, neither clergy nor laity. Placing all these offices under the heading of commissioned ministry might sort things out for working with the IRS and other government agencies, but so far as providing adequate definition for our workers and our churches, much work is left to be done to clarify the theological place of commissioned workers as they relate to the Office of Public Ministry.

CHAPTER 8

A Biblical Model

ACTS 6

> *Now in these days when the disciples were increasing in number, a complaint by the Hellenists arose against the Hebrews because their widows were being neglected in the daily distribution. And the twelve summoned the full number of the disciples and said, "It is not right that we should give up preaching the word of God to serve tables. Therefore, brothers, pick out from among you seven men of good repute, full of the Spirit and of wisdom, whom we will appoint to this duty. But we will devote ourselves to prayer and to the ministry of the word." And what they said pleased the whole gathering, and they chose Stephen, a man full of faith and of the Holy Spirit, and Philip, and Prochorus, and Nicanor, and Timon, and Parmenas, and Nicolaus, a proselyte of Antioch. These they set before the apostles, and they prayed and laid their hands on them.*
>
> *And the word of God continued to increase, and the number of the disciples multiplied greatly in Jerusalem, and a great many of the priests became obedient to the faith.* (Acts 6:1–7)

Following this story, other than Stephen and Philip, we do not hear more about the first deacons in the New Testament. We are left to wonder what their day-to-day service to the church might have been like. What did they really do as a part of their ministry? Are there aspects of their service to the church not discussed in Acts 6? What would a position description look like for these deacons? How did the apostles see the ministry of these deacons in relation to their own? Can we even justify calling what they did ministry? Didn't they just wait on tables?

These are just some of the questions that might be asked about this passage. When trying to understand a passage of Scripture such as this, it is important to begin by assessing what we are looking at. To begin with, Acts presents the history of the early church.

"Now in these days when the disciples were increasing in number, a complaint by the Hellenists arose against the Hebrews because their widows were being neglected in the daily distribution" (Acts 6:1). The church, according to Luke in Acts 6, was growing fast. Faster in fact than the apostles could keep up with. Due to this rapid growth, a disparity began to develop in the care being offered as part of the ministry of the congregation. The Hellenistic, or Greek, Jews began to note that their widows were not receiving equitable care. Hebraic Jewish widows were receiving disproportionate care when food was shared daily.

Perhaps the first point worth noting is that there was a daily food distribution. The early church considered a part of their ministry not only meeting the spiritual needs of their people, but also addressing their physical needs. Yet, it became clear to the apostles that the way in which this ministry was organized was not working as it ought.

"And the twelve summoned the full number of the disciples and said, "It is not right that we should give up preaching the word of God to serve tables" (Acts 6:2). The assessment of the apostles was that there were in fact two issues at hand. The first issue was the need for the Hellenistic widows to receive better care in the daily food distribution. The second issue was the need for the apostles themselves to avoid giving up too much of their time to solve the first issue themselves. It would seem from the text that the apostles may have begun to rectify the first issue on their own, only to realize the need for assistance.

Stott points out that the Twelve were not too busy to accomplish the ministry, but rather that they had focused on the wrong ministry.[1] Therefore, they called together the entire body of disciples in that place and sought to find a solution. Krodel argues that this is an example of how the church is called to respond to new challenges. The church is called to be responsive with new models of ministry that are better suited to respond to the developing needs of the people the church is called to serve.[2]

"Therefore, brothers, pick out from among you seven men of good repute, full of the Spirit and of wisdom, whom we will appoint to this duty. But we will devote ourselves to prayer and to the ministry of the word" (Acts 6:3–4). The question of how to address this situation might well have been handled by the apostles themselves. However, rather than simply making the decision by their own authority, the Twelve sought the input of the larger body of believers. The apostles asked the assembly, gathered together in perhaps one of the first voters' meetings, to select seven men from within their ranks to be put forward to serve on behalf of the whole congregation. These men were presented to the apostles for appointment to serve the church, laying hands on them as they placed these men into ministry.

This process is beneficial for the church today to understand, in that it demonstrates the wisdom of seeking the input of the whole church. By explaining the situation as they did, the apostles were able to avoid the accusation that their purpose was merely to avoid labor that was beneath them.[3] Rather, the purpose was to allow the apostles to return to their primary ministry.

"And what they said pleased the whole gathering, and they chose Stephen,

---

1 Stott, *The Spirit, the Church, and the World*, 123.

2 Krodel, *Acts*, 133.

3 Calvin, *The Acts of the Apostles*, 157.

a man full of faith and of the Holy Spirit, and Philip, and Prochorus, and Nicanor, and Timon, and Parmenas, and Nicolaus, a proselyte of Antioch" (Acts 6:5). Some, perhaps all, of the men listed in verse 5 were Greek Jews themselves, which speaks to the concerns not only to resolve the basic care situation but to do so while attempting to intentionally build or restore bridges within the community of believers.[4] These were men whom the people as a whole believed were full of spiritual maturity and wisdom. This was essential, but not merely for the purpose of handling food distribution. To think of their ministry as merely that of distributing food is to miss a larger point. The reason these men were selected in the manner that they were was in order that through their Holy Spirit–led wisdom, the community would be restored. It was not merely the apostles and their ministry of the Word that was needed to restore unity, but these men also were needed to set a tone that would restore solidarity among the believers across cultural lines.

"These they set before the apostles, and they prayed and laid their hands on them" (Acts 6:6). What is the significance of the laying on of hands in this particular instance? Some have suggested that this is a form of consecration or dedication for service to God.[5] Other suggest that this is a form of ordination[6] or commissioning.[7] Still others discuss the act of laying on hands from the perspective of the placing of these men in their new office.[8] Others still talk in terms of the transfer of power or authority from one individual or group to another.[9]

Regardless of the specific understanding of the text, something significant is taking place. There is a new office being established. But what is this office, and what is its relationship to the apostles? Though not directly mentioned, it is often surmised that these seven were the original deacons. Lutherans have typically seen a distinction between the ministry of the apostles and these deacons, and thus see a distinction between the ordination of elders and the commissioning of deacons. Yet, both are to be understood as ministerial offices.[10]

"And the word of God continued to increase, and the number of the disciples multiplied greatly in Jerusalem, and a great many of the priests became obedient to the faith" (Acts 6:7). In the final verse of this passage of Scripture,

---

4 Talbert, *Reading Acts: A Literary and Theological Commentary on the Acts of the Apostles,* 59–60.

5 Calvin, *The Acts of the Apostles*, 355.

6 Martin, Smith, and Oden, *Acts*, 71.

7 Talbert, *Reading Acts: A Literary and Theological Commentary on the Acts of the Apostles,* 60; Krodel, *Acts,* 133–34.

8 Stellhorn, *Annotations on the Acts of the Apostles,* 74; Lenski, *The Interpretation of the Acts of the Apostles,* 245.

9 Smith, *Concordia Commentary: Acts,* 112.

10 Walther, *The Church and the Office of the Ministry*, 284.

Luke points to the end result and therefore back to the purpose for the establishment of this new office. The church in Jerusalem continued to grow. By establishing a new office to assist the apostles, the growth taking place in the early church continued. Not only did the church continue to grow, but that growth was rapid. How the church is organized matters. What's more, Luke notes that a specific group of Jews came to believe in Jesus as the Christ. A number of Jewish priests confessed faith in Christ following the establishment of the office of the deacon. The deacons were not likely themselves responsible for the conversion of these priests, but their ministry allowed the apostles to continue their ministry.

DESCRIPTIVE NARRATIVE

What are we to do with the recounting of a story such as this? How is this narrative to inform the practice of the church in the twenty-first century? Acts is narrative history. Luke is attempting to provide for Theophilus, as well as centuries of readers since, with an orderly account of first what took place in the life and ministry of Jesus of Nazareth and second, in the book we call Acts, an account of the growth and expansion of the early church through the ministry of the apostles.

As a narrative, the passages under consideration ought to be taken first as a recounting of what took place. Only once this is understood ought we to attempt to derive principles for modern-day application from the text. Our modern tendency to see every passage of Scripture as the source for principles for daily living is a critical flaw in our understanding of the original intent of the text. One cannot simply reduce a story such as this to an argument that the church ought to have deacons today that are cast in the same form as those established by the apostles.

Rather, examining the text, one ought to be guided by its narrative structure. Therefore, the modern church ought to first learn about how the early church responded to a crisis. Secondarily, the modern church can then learn how a similar process might be employed to respond to new crises today. When considering passages on qualifications for elders and deacons (1 Timothy 3:1–7, 8–13; Titus 1:6–9), Paul says that these qualifications for church leaders are necessary; they are prescriptive. However, what we see in Acts 6 is Luke's descriptive account of how the apostles responded to the concerns raised by the Hellenistic Jews.

When considering how to treat passages from Acts or any other narrative passage, it is important to keep in mind that unless explicit instruction indicates the text is normative for church practice, it is more appropriate to treat the passage as a narrative that may inform church practice but that does not mandate its structure.[11] Thus, when examining Acts 6, while there is much

11 Fee and Stuart, *How to Read the Bible for All Its Worth*, 124.

to consider when establishing or maintaining the practice of ministry in the church, the passage ought not to be taken as prescriptive, but rather as a description of what historically took place. The narrative of Acts 6 is descriptive of what took place, not prescriptive for what offices are mandated for the church today.

Much is made by some that the offices of the early church were defined rather than fluid.[12] This argument seems to focus on ensuring that there is no confusion between the service provided by deacons and the ministry of Word and Sacrament carried out by the apostles and those they ordained to follow them in ministry as pastors. The latter work of Stephen and Philip is therefore seen as either evidence that they transitioned into another office or a personal, non-public ministry beyond their diaconal office.[13]

The claim that taking on a more pastoral role would not have been a part of their office and citing a lack of biblical evidence to that effect makes sense up to a point. However, this line of argumentation works both for and against these claims. The lack of biblical evidence that deacons were called to do more than handling food distribution is accompanied by a similar lack of biblical discussion on such a restriction. We are simply told what they were commissioned to do. It might make better logical sense to argue that since there is no corresponding description of an expansion of those duties, that therefore there must not have been, yet this lacks certainty. We are dealing with competing arguments from silence.

Again, keeping in mind that we are dealing with a descriptive narrative is important. We have Luke's description of the call of these deacons, along with his descriptions of the further ministry of Philip and Stephen. What we do not have is any direct explanation either way with respect to the nature of the authority by which they continued to serve the kingdom beyond the initial diaconal duties.

The text is silent. Any assertions, one way or the other, require some element of extrapolation beyond the text itself. What you can say from the text is that both Philip and Stephen in some ways acted beyond their initial calling as deacons. Was there a new laying on of hands that preceded this expansion of their ministry? We do not know.

PRESCRIPTIVE INSTRUCTIONS

When we turn to look at texts like 1 Timothy 3:1–13 and Titus 1:6–9 (figure 12), we find that we are dealing with something quite different than the Acts 6 narrative. Paul is not telling a story to his young protégés, Timothy and Titus, about how he handled similar situations in his ministry as illustrations

---

12 Lenski, *The Interpretation of the Acts of the Apostles*, 247.

13 Marquart, *The Church and Her Fellowship, Ministry, and Governance*, 140; Krodel, *Acts*, 133–34; Lenski, *The Interpretation of the Acts of the Apostles*, 247.

for them to learn from. He very well could have done so, but that is not the approach he takes. Rather in both cases, Paul provides specific instructions, intending that these two young pastors and those who followed them take and make direct use of these instructions in their own pastorates.

FIGURE 12

1 TIMOTHY 3:1–7—OVERSEERS	1 TIMOTHY 3:8–13—DEACONS	TITUS 1:6–9—ELDERS
above reproach	blameless	blameless
faithful to his wife	husband of one wife	faithful to his wife
temperate		not overbearing
self-controlled		self-controlled
respectable	dignified	upright, holy and disciplined
hospitable		hospitable
able to teach		
not given to drunkenness	not addicted to much wine	not given to drunkenness
not violent but gentle		not violent
not quarrelsome		not quick-tempered
not a lover of money	not greedy for dishonest gain	not pursuing dishonest gain
manage his own family well	wives likewise must be dignified	
see that his children obey	managing their children and their own households well	children believe and are not open to the charge of being wild and disobedient
not be a recent convert	tested first	hold firmly to the trustworthy message as it has been taught
good reputation with outsiders		
	not double-tongued	

Comparing the passages, overlap can be seen. Merging the lists together, the church is provided with a fairly comprehensive list of qualities to look for in a church worker. It is interesting that in the 1 Timothy passages Paul addresses both overseers and deacons, while in Titus he simply addresses elders. Keeping in mind that overseers and elders can be considered equivalent to the modern pastor, it is intriguing that only one of the lists includes teaching. When we think about the modern pastoral office, teaching is often seen as integral. This does not mean that Paul is suggesting elders did not teach, but it is interesting to note the differing emphases in the lists in this and other qualifications.

FURTHER SCRIPTURAL DISCUSSION

In Ephesians 4:11, Paul provides a list of offices from the early church. This list is at times argued to consist of a combination of offices no longer in existence today (apostle and prophet) and those of the modern pastor (evangelist, shepherd, and teacher).[14] Above, it was pointed out that the modern understanding of a teacher, even a Lutheran teacher, ought not to be obfuscated in such a way as to claim that the teacher in Ephesians 4 and the classroom teacher are one and the same office.

Rather than seeing the modern teacher, some see the phrase "shepherds and teachers" as a single office, that of the pastor. Lutherans have been nothing if not consistent in their insistence upon there being a single office of ministry, yet simply rolling all New Testament offices together does not accomplish this. Rather, this line of argumentation moves beyond the necessity of the text, to provide a protection for the pastoral office in a way that unnecessarily eliminates those helping or auxiliary offices that have since the early church served to work with those in the pastoral office.

Zimmerman sees in the one article applied to both shepherds and teachers not a single office (shepherd-teacher), but rather ministers (pastors and teachers) from the same group, serving a congregation together.[15] Both Zimmerman and Kähler suggest the possibility that the "teachers" reference could be catechist.[16] There is, however, a way of looking at the text and not having to either equivocate the two or only uphold the pastoral office. In the case where a local congregation is served by a single man as pastor, the entire Office of the Public Ministry resides in his office as pastor. In the case where a catechist or other office bearer works alongside the pastor, that additional individual serves in a branch or helping office. This latter example does not take away from the pastoral office in any way, nor does it suggest that the work done by the bearer of the helping office is somehow less than that done by the pastor. The helping office may not be the sole bearer of the Office of the Public Ministry in the way that the pastor may. The helping office ought always to seek to uplift the work done from the pastoral office. This is what Walther was getting at in *The Church and the Office of the Ministry* when he lists schoolteachers among others as ones "which bear a part of the one church office."[17]

F. C. D. Wyneken saw something further in Ephesians 4:11. While much is made about the distinction between pastors and teachers, Wyneken focused

---

14 Mayes, Robert, "'Equipping the Saints'?: Why Ephesians 4:11–12 Opposes the Theology and Practice of Lay Ministry," 9–10.

15 Zimmerman, "The Lutheran Teacher: Minister of the Church – Revisited," 272.

16 Kähler, "Does a Congregation Ordinarily Have the Right Temporarily to Commit an Essential Part of the Holy Preaching Office to a Layman," 40.

17 Walther, *The Church and the Office of the Ministry*, 286.

on the role of the evangelist, going so far as to support the establishment of a called position for the synod to support his passion for mission work in North America. While the LCMS opted in convention not to establish the position of evangelist, had they done so those called to this role would have served as an additional office of ministry offering support for the preaching office. Like the office of teacher (modern day or ancient catechist), an office of evangelist would be a branch office of the Office of Public Ministry.

Interestingly, in 1 Timothy, Paul provides an indication that not all elders are elders who preach. "Let the elders who rule well be considered worthy of double honor, especially those who labor in preaching and teaching" (1 Timothy 5:17). Recalling that the biblical use of the term *elder* is more equivalent to the modern pastor than laypeople serving as elders in the church today, this passage often goes unnoticed in this discussion. Paul distinguished between elders who rule, that is exercise authority, and those who preach and teach. Once again, this does not mean that there is more than one Office of the Public Ministry, but it does provide further evidence that a proper understanding of this office is not exclusive to the office of the pastor.

SUGGESTING A BIBLICAL MODEL

Rather than seeing what took place in Acts 6 as a prescription for the number and types of offices that the church is to have today, and keeping in mind the descriptive nature of the passage, Luke is providing an example for the church to follow. When faced with circumstances where a pastor is in need of help in his ministry, other offices suited to provide that help may be established in a manner similar to that described in Acts. The lists of offices from the New Testament, along with the description of the manner in which the apostles established the office of deacon, does not limit; it instructs. The church throughout history and even today must, at times, adapt in order to best respond to the needs of ministry in the local church as well as in the larger church body. Just as the apostles established the office of deacon to allow them to focus on preaching the Gospel, the LCMS has established commissioned ministry roles. Similarly, just as the early church selected seven to serve among them as deacons, congregations call individuals to serve in ministries in support of the work of the pastor.

For Luther understood Acts 6 in this manner; he held that

> Again, we even read in Acts [6:1–6] regarding an even lesser office, that the apostles were not permitted to institute persons as deacons without the knowledge and consent of the congregation. Rather, the congregation elected and called the seven deacons, and the apostles confirmed them. If, then, the apostles were not permitted to institute, on their own authority, an office having to do only with the distribution of temporal food, how could they have dared to impose the highest office of preach-

> ing on anyone by their own power without the knowledge, will, and call of the congregation?[18]

The establishment of the deacons, though guided by the apostles, was done by the authority of the congregation assembled, not merely by the apostles.

The structure and manner in which we organize those who serve in church ministry was not prescribed in total in the New Testament. The pastor is clearly identified and divinely established. The diaconate of the early church was established by the apostles through the guidance of the Holy Spirit and with the blessing of the church. This does not make the work of the diaconate less than divine. The way in which the deacons were selected and set aside by the laying on of hands, gives a good indication that their work was seen as public ministry. This public ministry was on behalf of the full number of the disciples, that is, the apostles asked these seven to assist them, placing them in public service to the Body of Christ in Jerusalem. Yet with the appointment of the deacons, the church had raised up a new office that branched from the Office of the Public Ministry to assist the apostles in their public ministry.

Using this model, the church has raised up new offices that branch from the Office of the Public Ministry to serve their own public ministry. Each new era in the church necessitates a new look at how the church structures its ministry. The core that is the one Office of the Public Ministry remains and must remain, but those offices that branch from it are an element of Christian liberty for the church to solemnly establish.

18 LW 39:312.

CHAPTER 9

A Theology of Commissioned Ministry

Introduction

Through the previous chapters, the foundation has been laid in order to set the stage for the final argument of this book. In this final chapter, the various streams, scriptural, historical, and practical, will be drawn together in an attempt to outline a way forward. The focus finally is to lay out a theology of commissioned ministry.

The first disciples were directly called by Jesus to leave behind all they had known and follow. They had Christ, there, right in front of them, to guide and to instruct them. For three years, they followed, they listened, and they learned. In the end, Jesus fulfilled the prophecies they had heard since childhood. Jesus was indeed the Christ, and through His perfect life, death, and resurrection, the disciples and all who were to follow His teaching down through the ages were restored to a right relationship with the Father.

Following some final instruction, Jesus took the disciples out to the mount called Olivet, and there departed this earth. Ascending to heaven, Jesus left his disciples to spread His Word to the entire world. Yet, to do this, they would need help.

After Pentecost, freshly empowered by the Holy Spirit, the mission to bring the Gospel to Judea, Samaria, and the ends of the earth began in earnest for the disciples. Initially, they restored their number with the selection of Matthias to replace Judas, who had betrayed Christ. Then in Acts 6, others were set aside to serve the community as deacons. Elsewhere in the New Testament, we hear of elders, bishops, and perhaps deaconesses (if that is what was being eluded to in Romans 16:1 in reference to Phoebe). Further, we hear about "the apostles, the prophets, the evangelists, the shepherds and teachers" in Ephesians 4:11. We even are provided with qualifications for overseers, elders, and deacons in 1 Timothy 3:1–13 and Titus 1:6–9. But the question remains whether this is to be taken as a definitive list, if these enumerated roles are all to be understood as slight changes of the pastoral office, and whether the church of today is able to or even should make its own adjustments to the offices of the ministry in order to better respond to the needs of the people they serve.

In the previous chapter, the argument was laid out that what took place in

Acts 6 should be taken as a description of those events rather than a prescription for how the church ought to approach the establishment of non-pastoral offices and the relationship of those offices to the pastoral office. Just as the apostles determined that a need was not being meet, so the church today may at times establish new offices in order to respond to needs that may not best be handled by pastors. In larger congregations, there may exist not only the need for additional pastors, but for others who specialize in particular areas of ministry in support of the ministry of the pastor(s). The development of our LCMS school system necessitates the formation of Lutheran teachers to support its educational ministry. While there are a good number of pastors who serve in part or in full in our LCMS schools, we set up special training for our teachers to meet the specific needs of this educational ministry.

This has taken place in the case of each area of commissioned ministry. A case had to be made before the synod in convention to demonstrate the necessity for each classification of worker. Unlike the pastoral office, which was directly and divinely established and is the one necessary office for the church, the creation of each of these commissioned ministry classifications are optional offices that the church is able in Christian freedom to both establish and disestablish in like manner. However, if a classification of commissioned ministry were to be disestablished, a similar case should be made to justify the cessation of that ministry office. Such an argument might be that the need, which prompted the creation of the classification, no longer exists or is not adequately served by the particular classification of worker.

CLARIFYING TERMS

Throughout this book, the terms "Office of the Public Ministry" and "Priesthood of All Believers" have been discussed. As was previously made clear, all Christians are a part of the Priesthood of All Believers. Pastors are members of the Priesthood of All Believers called to serve the laity (those not called into public ministry); they are bearers of the Office of the Public Ministry.

As noted above, commissioned ministers do not always feel properly at home in either category, clergy or laity. When the Office of the Public Ministry is seen as synonymous with the pastoral office, commissioned ministers rightly understand that this would not include them. Yet, when the term *laity* is used to distinguish those in the church, who are members of the Priesthood of All Believers and not ordained as pastors, commissioned ministers are left excluded as well.

Laity can be defined as distinct from clergy or alternatively as distinct from experts. Called workers, both ordained and commissioned, by nature of their training (both theological and ministry-area specific) should be considered experts. Typically, this is not the sense in which the clergy/laity distinction is used within the church. However, the DPM ought to be seen as a distinctly Lutheran expert in church music because of the training received. Many women in the local congregation should be encouraged to assist the pastor in caring for other women in the congregation, but the deaconess by her theological and care-ministry training should be seen as an expert. This distinction holds for our called Lutheran teachers, whose theological training should distinguish them from other hired teachers, who may well be good and faithful Christians but who have not been theologically prepared to approach the teaching craft with an informed Lutheran theology.

One of the purposes of having commissioned ministers is to have theologically trained individuals who can faithfully assist the pastor in carrying out the ministry of the congregation. These workers receive training specific to their calls and many times seek further training to enhance their skill set. In the same way, the apostles recognized that while they might have been able to serve the widows of the church in Jerusalem, they called others through the authority of the congregation and placed them in offices to carry out this vital service, allowing them to return to the preaching of the Gospel.

Being called by the church to serve, having been called out of the laity in order to serve, ought to distinguish commissioned ministers from the laity, just as ordination distinguishes the clergy. Yet at this point, commissioned ministers are still often defined only by what they are not. In order to provide the groundwork for a definition of commissioned ministers based on what they are rather than what they are not, there is a need to understand first the terms used prior to our modern use of "commissioned."

Walther's *The Church and the Ministry*, officially adopted by the LCMS in 1851, notes that auxiliary offices are "holy offices, which bear a part of the one church office."[1] There are some in both the LCMS and WELS who view the use of the term *auxiliary* as unfortunate, but for different reasons. For some in the WELS, the concern seems to be that this term lowers the view of those who hold such offices. For some in the LCMS, the concern seems to be that this term overly elevates such offices, causing confusion with the pastoral office.

Yet when understood as a helping office, auxiliary offices should not be seen as either at risk of usurping the pastoral office, nor denigrated to the extent that they are not considered to have a place within the Office of the Public Ministry. As previously noted, Walther held to the divinity of the teacher's office.[2] Pastors and teachers were colleagues, but they were not to confuse who was in which office.

Lehenbauer wrestles with the distinctions, noting that the offices of commissioned workers are both divine and human. "Those who hold the office of

---

1 Walther, *The Church and the Office of the Ministry*, 286.

2 Wohlrabe, "An Historical Analysis of the Doctrine of the Ministry in The Lutheran Church—Missouri Synod," 64.

DCE have a *divine* call and carry out a variety of *divinely instituted* functions."[3] Lehenbauer further notes that "The office of DCE as such is *humanly* instituted, i.e. instituted by the church."[4]

Matthew Harrison (the thirteenth president of the LCMS) discusses Thesis IV on the church of Walther's *The Church and the Office of the Ministry,* noting that "(A)ll together possess all the offices of the church. Since the Office of the Ministry belongs to all, no one has the right to assume its duties publicly unless by appointment of the whole."[5] Thus, I, as a DCE, ought not to assume ministry role of my own volition, but rather serve because of my external call as a DCE. Harrison cites Chemnitz, stating that:

> Finally, since one minister does not suffice for a large number of people or an entire city, it is the duty of the church administrators to ordain and appoint others as deacons, pastors, or fellow office bearers. Among these there should be a certain order or rank so that, for the furtherance of the salvation of the believers and for the strengthening of the kingdom of Christ, all things shall be done decently and in order.[6]

Note that there are two possible solutions to the struggle of a pastor needing additional assistance with the work of ministry. First, the congregation may call an additional pastor to share the load. Second, the congregation may call a deacon. The concept of the auxiliary or helping office stems from the diaconal office, and thus we can see in Chemnitz a rationale for calling specialized office bearers who assist the pastor by taking on areas of ministry that allow the pastor to remain focused on the proclamation of the Gospel.

Harrison argues in support for referring to auxiliary offices as helping offices:

> For Walther, the presence of "helping offices" (a better term than "auxiliary office" in my view) expresses the Church's freedom to create such offices as need requires. The aspect of the parochial schoolteacher that Walther emphasizes in this respect is the "teaching of the Word of God" to young people. The tension that often exists between pastor and teacher are in some large measure the result of our collapse of all terms for the Office of the Ministry and all other office in the church into general "ministry" . . . The pastor has the preaching office. This office is an office of service. The teacher—so far as he or she teaches the Word of God—has an office that assists and is responsible to the pastor in this task. Teachers have a churchly, diaconal (that is, serving or ministering) office.[7]

---

3 Lehenbauer, *Equipping the Saints*, 49.

4 Lehenbauer, *Equipping the Saints*, 49.

5 Walther, *The Church and the Office of the Ministry*, 36.

6 Walther, *The Church and the Office of the Ministry*, 48.

7 Walther, *The Church and the Office of the Ministry*, 284.

Harrison does not argue that such helping offices are not to be seen as having a place within the Office of the Public Ministry. Rather, he argues that they are not interchangeable with the Office of the Public Ministry, and they are not "general ministry." This is where A. C. Stellhorn and A. C. Mueller went awry in the 1960s. Articulating a position in which the pastoral office was merely one of many expressions of the Office of the Public Ministry was a denigration of the pastoral or preaching office.

Walther's Thesis VIII on the Office states that "The preaching office [Predigtamt] is the highest office in the Church, from which flow all other offices in the Church."[8] One cannot hold that the preaching office is both merely one of many and at the same time hold the preaching office up as the highest office. Likewise, one cannot hold that the preaching office is the highest office and at the same time hold that all other offices are not a part of the public ministry.

It may help at this point to further clarify what is meant by public ministry. Public ministry is perhaps best understood in contrast to private ministry. All members of the Priesthood of All Believers have a private ministry. All Christians are empowered by the Holy Spirit to speak the Gospel both to those outside and those inside the church.

All Christians are able to speak words of comfort and forgiveness on behalf of God. Thus, private ministry is done by every member of the Priesthood without an office created or designated by the church. For example, as a father, I am called to bring God's Word to my sons and as a husband to my wife. I am called to speak the Gospel to them and to remind them of the forgiveness that is theirs in Christ. My authority to serve my family is not an authority granted by or for the church. This is a private ministry.

In contrast, the Office of the Public Ministry was established in a different way and for a different purpose than the office of parent. The Office of the Public Ministry is the office created to serve on behalf of the Body of Christ gathered locally in a congregation or recognized service organization (RSO) of a church body like the LCMS. Therefore, the point of differentiation between private and public is on whose behalf the ministry is done.

When the pastor and other ministers serve by God's authority as given to the congregation and on behalf of God and the church in a designated office, that is public ministry. Public ministry is not that which is done "publicly," in front of others. Rather, the "on behalf of" nature of the call from the church makes the ministry public. The proclamation of the Gospel in worship on Sunday morning is a public ministry not because it can be witnessed by many people in an accessible setting (increasingly more so with the advent of livestreaming). The declaration of forgiveness by the pastor is a public ministry because he has been placed by the congregation in his office to make that declaration.

---

8 Walther, *The Church and the Office of the Ministry*, 284.

In like manner, the public nature of the call of helping office bearers, such as the commissioned ministers of the LCMS, places them in a form of public ministry particular to the nature of their call. The Lutheran teacher is placed in a public ministry to instruct her students in accordance with Scripture and the Lutheran Confessions. The DCE is placed in a public ministry to provide for the Christian education of members of the congregation (individual calls may provide for a full life-span approach or a specific age-restricted responsibility).

The ministry of the deaconess may not always take place in a public setting. Caring for the dying may be a very one-on-one ministry. However, this is a public ministry because it is done on behalf of the church.

Lehenbauer states that

> DCE's are at the *intersection* of these two offices/vocations. As Christ "bridged" the gap between God and man with His two natures, DCE's are uniquely positioned to bridge the gap between the OPM and the PAB through the "two natures" of their office for the dual purpose of *assisting* and *supporting* the pastoral office and *equipping* the saints.[9]

This applies to all commissioned ministers. Like all believers, commissioned ministers are a part of the Priesthood of All Believers. As public ministers, their ministry is a part of the Office of the Public Ministry, though as noted previously the offices of commissioned minister are not *the* Office of the Public Ministry.

Thus, commissioned ministers have a place within the Office of the Public Ministry as specified in the call of the congregation and sanctioned by the LCMS as a whole. The intersection of the "Office of Public Ministry Turnpike" and the "Royal Priesthood Parkway" therefore does not imply some kind of no-man's land as has been the perceived view of many (pastors, commissioned, and laity alike). This intersection, as we have seen, places the commissioned minister firmly in both camps. Perhaps the advantage of the commissioned minister is the dual nature of his or her call. There is perhaps a closeness to both pastors and the laity. Rather than seeing the ministry of the commissioned minister for what it is not, it would be better to see the validity that these offices have in their own right. All called workers find their place somewhere in this intersection. Being a pastor does not remove a man from his role as a part of the royal priesthood. However, to Lehenbauer's point, the perception of those called to be pastors is such that there appears to be less of a connection to the laity who remain entirely on the "Royal Priesthood Parkway."

There is, however, a need to clarify our language. When pastors and others talk to male commissioned workers about whether they have considered "the ministry," the validity of commissioned ministry is undermined. While it may be a worthy compliment to suggest that a male commissioned worker may

9 Lehenbauer, *Equipping the Saints*, 60.

well be suited for pastoral ministry, to suggest that his current office is neither a public ministry nor a part of the Office of Public Ministry is to have a low view of his current service. When we talk about the church as being made up of clergy and laity (or as was heard at the Pacific Southwest District Convention proclaimers and hearers), the validity of commissioned ministry is undermined. When terms like "church worker" are used to refer to only pastors (as has been seen related to debt-reduction campaigns for pastors), our language undermines the validity of commissioned ministry. These may not be intentional acts, but they have an impact.

THE SERVICE OF WOMEN AS COMMISSIONED MINISTERS

The focus on this book has not been to argue a case for the ministry of women, yet a case cannot be made for the public ministry of commissioned ministers without acknowledging the place of women in that ministry. Scripture is clear that God has given the responsibility of pastoral ministry to men. Scripture is equally clear that there is a place for the service of women. We need only think of Deborah the prophetess (Judges 4) or Phoebe (Roman 16) to know that there is a place for the ministry of women in the church. However, this does not equate to a calling to a headship role as pastor.

Much of the ministry of women noted in the Bible fits comfortably within the helping offices construct under discussion here. Yet, if there is going to be an agreement to include commissioned ministers as bearers of a public office of ministry, a case needs to be made to either include or exclude women serving in those roles.

As a husband, I have a certain headship that my wife does not have within my family. This does not take away from her parental vocation; it merely distinguishes responsibility before God. Just as ordination does not confer some "unchangeable, indelible character on the man,"[10] the headship of the husband in the family does not have its source in some indelible character of the man lacking in the woman. In a like manner, the headship of the pastor, being preserved in the understanding of the relationship between the preaching office and the helping offices, does not necessitate a complete lack of ministerial office for women. It merely restricts to those helping offices that at no time may bear the full Office of the Public Ministry.

Gärtner observes that "(w)hen considering the relationship of man and woman, and especially the relationship of woman and the office, it is of basic importance that the principle of 'subordination' be considered."[11] Brunner outlines Luther's view in this way:

> Luther had a very unequivocal answer to the question whether or not women should be called to the pastoral office, which can be summarized under the following points:

---

10 Walther, *The Church and the Office of the Ministry*, 151.

11 Gärtner, "Didaskalos: The Office, Man, and Woman in the New Testament," 30.

All Christians have the spiritual power to proclaim the Word of God, and that includes women.

1. In the assembled congregation, only he may preach the Word who has been called to do so by the church.
2. Only he may be called who has the ability.
3. In determining whether one possesses the ability, spiritual and natural factors must be considered.
4. The subordination of the woman to the man, as has been established in the Old Testament, has not been revoked in the New Testament; rather it has been substantiated by the Holy Spirit through the pronouncement of the apostles.
5. The Holy Spirit would contradict Himself if He allowed women to preach in the services of the congregation as long as there were men present whom he has inspired thereto.
6. The *ordo*, which must be maintained, has a spiritual character, it is the work of the Holy Spirit. The moral attitude that corresponds to this *ordo* is propriety. Neither the *ordo* nor its corresponding sense of propriety dare be violated.
7. As long as the presupposition holds true that there are men present whom the Holy Spirit has inspired to preach, it is not proper for the woman to be called to exercise the pastoral office.
8. One can safely assume that the Holy Spirit, in keeping with his directives in the Holy Scriptures, will see to it that capable men are not lacking. Should this unusual circumstance nevertheless prevail, then—but only then—must women also preach in the services of the congregation.[12]

In the extreme or emergency situations,[13] it does appear that while Luther does not advocate aspiring to the office he does advocate fulfilling the duty of the office. What is not stated, however, is any sense in which all aspects of public ministry are excluded. Just as with male commissioned ministers, female commissioned ministers are to keep their ministry under the headship of the pastor. Women, as well as men, are called to proclaim the Gospel. Both

12 Brunner, "The Ministry and the Ministry of Women," 268–69.

13 It is beyond the scope of this work to define the specific criteria that are to be employed to demarcate when an unusual circumstance might be considered in effect. Factors such as geographic isolation and pastoral availability do factor in. However, unless outright impossible, the guidance of pastoral oversight should be followed even during such times.

may proclaim that Gospel by virtue of their being commissioned workers and a part of the Office of Public Ministry. However, their public ministry, just like all commissioned ministry, must be kept distinct from the full Office of the Public Ministry. Women serving as DCEs, Lutheran teachers, or any other helping office remain along with their male counterparts under that headship of the pastor, who alone is entrusted with the full Office of the Public Ministry and is not to claim otherwise. Commissioned workers are to exercise only the specific ministry related to their training and calling.[14]

WALKING TOGETHER

As a church body, we attempt to walk together on a number of issues included in our theology and practice. One of these is our use of rostered workers. Our churches and schools may not always be consistent in practice, but a part of being in the LCMS ought to be an emphasis on the use of called workers wherever possible. There are times and situations when this is not an option. There may be unique factors that prevent a church or school from calling a rostered worker to serve. However, this ought to be the exception. The practice of simply hiring a lay person to handle the functions of a particular area of ministry imports a functionalism into our theology of the call that is foreign to our understanding of ministry.

Discussing Walther's Thesis VI on the Church, Harrison states:

> I believe it is self-evident from the material below that while a "synod" carries out all sorts of tasks and functions that may not be essential to the existence of the Church, nevertheless a synod is in fact "church" because it is a transcongregational expression of ecclesiastical unity (church fellowship).[15]

In ecclesiastical unity, the LCMS selects which helping offices are to be established and for what purpose. When necessary, the local congregation may hire lay workers to handle similar work, but this is to be distinguished from the ministry done by those who bear the offices that the LCMS as a "transcongregational" entity elects to establish. Where possible, training leading to becoming a commissioned minister should be encouraged by the local congregation or school.

The calling of specific men and women to serve as Lutheran teachers, Directors of Christian Education, deaconesses, Lay Ministers, Directors of Family Life Ministry, Directors of Christian Outreach, and Directors of Parish Music has been sanctioned by the synod. Therefore congregations are to be encouraged to add those helping ministers to their ministries that best extend the work of the local church. Chemnitz noted:

---

14 See Chapter 1 for details on each commissioned ministry.

15 Walther, *The Church and the Office of the Ministry,* 65.

> Luther taught from the Word of God that Christ gave and committed the Keys, that is, the office of the Word and Sacraments, to the whole Church . . . so that the highest power of the Word and of the Sacraments is with God; then, that the office belongs to the Church, through which God mediately calls, chooses, and sends ministers.[16]

It is in the end the local church who under the guidance of their church body selects and calls men into the pastoral office and both men and women into the helping offices of commissioned ministry. Together we are called to respect one another's vocations and talents. We ought to lift one another up, not seek to supplant one another or lord any authority that we have been given by God through the church over one another.

Put into a practical setting, this means that the local teacher or DCE does not have the right to publicly counter the teaching of the pastor without great care and communication with the pastor on the points of disagreement. This does not mean that there will not be such points of interpretive dissonance, but rather that, being in an auxiliary office, these office bearers are called to not publicly undermine the ministry of the Word without due process and to address the points of disagreement privately.

Further, the church musician is not in an office that would allow for an alteration of the nature of worship that is not in accord with the studied understanding of the pastor. The introduction of new music and other elements of worship are to be done with the blessing of the pastor and with his full support.

Though not necessarily directly addressed, one could extend this concept to include the manner in which those in commissioned offices are to support the vision and leadership of the pastor in the local church. There is a reason that it is not typical to call auxiliary workers to a congregation during a time of pastoral vacancy. In the circumstance of a commissioned minister, when judging if a call extended to him by a congregation may be accepted, he may determine what agreement and congruence exists between his own approach to ministry and the approach of the pastor.

If a DCE already called to a congregation is unable to support the vision of the pastor, his role is not to undermine the ministry of this pastor; he may determine that considering taking another call would serve the larger church. This may also happen when a new pastor is called to a congregation already served by a commissioned worker. Those in auxiliary ministry should not undermine the congregation's call, which seeks a pastor with a vision akin to her own.

Even in the case that the vision of the pastor and the larger congregation are not in accord, it is not the proper place of the commissioned minister to

---

16 Walther, *The Church and the Office of the Ministry*, 86.

publicly advocate against the vision of the pastor or direction of the congregation. For example, a DCE may have objections to holding Sunday School at the same time as worship on a Sunday morning due to the dividing of families for both worship and Christian education, while the pastor may see the necessity for this arrangement in order to seek more of the lost for Christ. If, after good faith efforts on the part of the pastor and commissioned minister to reach an accord, they determine that their visions for ministry are in fact non-compatible, it is the proper place for the commissioned minister to begin to seek a call to serve in another setting. Even in the case that the vision of the pastor and the larger congregation are not in accord, it is not the proper place of the commissioned minister to publicly advocate against the vision of the pastor.

All that said, the pastor should at all times show due respect and speak highly of the other called workers in the congregation and school. Every opportunity should be taken to lift up the work of the Lutheran teacher, DCE, DPM, or principal. Working together as colleagues and true partners in service goes a long way to making for a fruitful ministry.

Recently, a local pastor and DCE spoke in a class preparing church workers. When discussing how they function together in ministry, the pastor stated that he begins by treating the DCE and other called staff as equals. The DCE followed this by noting that he in return follows the lead of his pastor. That is how team ministry is to be properly approached. From the senior position, the pastor shares generously of his authority. From the junior position, other called workers assume the role to support and follow the pastor's lead. They work together seeking the best for the congregation. They freely disagree in staff meetings and in private, yet publicly they are a unified voice in mission and ministry.

SO, WHAT IS A COMMISSIONED MINISTER?

The proposed answer to the question stated above, "How does the auxiliary nature of these offices relate to the Office of Public Ministry?" can be found across the discussion of the Office of the Public Ministry in this book. Borrowing a bit of philosophical language,[17] I would outline the question this way: If the pastoral office is coextensive with the preaching office, then commissioned ministers are not within the Office of the Public Ministry; however, the church has the freedom to create other helping offices and to call people to them as public ministers in a derivative sense. If, on the other hand, the pastoral office is not coextensive with the preaching office, then we can understand commissioned ministers as being within the public ministry but still in a helping sense, as the office of pastor is the only office within the public ministry which Christ specifically instituted and which is not optional for congregations.

17 I am thankful to my colleague David Loy for this language. It is very helpful in framing the concepts under consideration.

Drawing upon the understanding of Acts 6 and other passages put forth above, along with a review of Luther and our Lutheran fathers, it seems clear that the pastoral office is not coextensive with the office of preaching. Commissioned ministers stand beside the preaching office in holy offices "which bear a part of the one church office."[18] Lutheran teachers, DCEs, DCOs, DPMs, deaconesses, DFLMs, and called Lay Ministers are not a part of the laity. The rostering of Lay Ministers adds to the confusion of this issue. Properly speaking, if one understands commissioned ministers to work alongside pastors and not as laity, then the term "Lay Minster" should be considered an oxymoron. This does not denigrate the ministry of those called into this ministry, but rather merely points out that they ought not be called a Lay Minister any more than someone ought to be called a Lay DCE or Lay Teacher.

Returning to the definition of the Office of Public Ministry used previously, if the Office of Public Ministry can be defined as those called by the Priesthood of All Believers to serve in ministry on their behalf, then we can state the following. In the case where there is only a pastor, then the full Office of the Public Ministry is placed upon him. In the case where there are multiple pastors or multiple called workers, the senior pastor is still entrusted with the full Office of Public Ministry, bearing the full responsibility for those called to serve under him, while all others are called to share the Office of Public Ministry but not bear it in total. This does not place the associate pastor and commissioned workers in the same category, as the associate pastor remains a pastor just as the senior pastor is a pastor. But rather, the responsibility for the entirety of the ministry is not placed upon the associate pastor, whereas this would not be done except in emergency or unusual circumstances with the commissioned worker.

Like the pastor, commissioned ministers are members of the Priesthood of All Believers called to serve in the various church vocations that have been established in the LCMS. These holy offices are divine, not because Christ specifically ordained their creation or because they are mentioned directly in Scripture, but rather because their public ministry is a true part of the Office of the Public Ministry that was established by Christ.

COMMISSIONED VOTING

It would not be proper to have raised the question of commissioned ministers voting in district and synodical conventions and not come back to resolve that discussion. While this is a more practical and perhaps political matter, it does speak to the lack of recognition that commissioned workers have within the LCMS.

To start, commissioned workers are clearly not a part of the laity, and to place them in that capacity for a convention is both a confusion theologically

---

18 Walther, *The Church and the Office of the Ministry*, 286.

as well as a muting of the proper voice of the laity in the leadership of the synod. As noted above, the dual role of the commissioned worker as one found on the intersection of the "Office of Public Ministry Turnpike" and the "Royal Priesthood Parkway" is universal to all called workers. Therefore the commissioned minister is no more a part of the laity than the pastor is, just as the commissioned worker is no more a pastor than the laity are. However, though one might draw the conclusion that since commissioned workers are a part of the Office of the Public Ministry that they are represented by those bearing the full office—namely, pastors—I would argue instead that due to the distinct nature of who commissioned ministers are they ought to be provided a voice[19] of their own and some element of voting representation. In order to accomplish this a third category for voting delegate should be established that would seek to take away neither from the vote of pastors nor the laity.

Using the same rationale that the synod did to determine the need to establish each office, it would seem clear that having these distinct voices adds tremendous value not only to local ministry, but to the larger discussions related to the direction of the LCMS. The LCMS functions at a deficit without these voices joining together with our pastors and laity in shaping our ministry together. The specific mechanics on how this might be done are best left to be wrestled out in future conventions. It is, however, critical that we understand that we are a better synod because of the service of all our church workers, and our conventions would be better informed by a similar inclusion of vision and viewpoint.

CARE FOR COMMISSIONED MINISTERS

There is a growing need for better care for all the workers serving the church. The pressures of our culture are increasingly hostile to service as a church worker. The LCMS is in theory structured to both provide supervision as well as care for its congregations, schools, and church workers. However, in practice this effort stops short of what it could or perhaps should be.

There have been districts that have provided retreats for pastors and their wives. How many have considered offering a similar event for commissioned workers and spouses? Gender differences make the work more complex, but having spent plenty of time talking with the husbands of commissioned workers, there is a need to help them support their church worker wife just as much as pastor's wife, even if that support looks different.

---

19 The astute reader may have noticed that I may be conflating voice and vote as though one is synonymous with the other. While commissioned workers do officially have a voice in conventions as advisory delegates, as they are able to speak from the floor on topic under discussion, I would argue that this voice is greatly lacking for two reasons. (1) A voice without vote bears with it little substance to impact the course of convention business. (2) Functionally, the voice of commissioned workers is relegated to the back of the room and routinely overlooked to ensure microphone time for voting delegates.

Districts that hold new pastor orientations ought to consider expanding this to include all called workers. Those with large numbers of new workers may consider offering different kinds of orientations, though there is a benefit to all workers seeing one another and honoring the ministry that each is called to. All-worker conferences may also be an approach that could seek to bring workers together and develop greater mutual support and understanding.[20] Casting a vision for ministry together at such a conference may go a long way.

Circuit visitors are generally well prepared to care for their fellow pastors. The 2016 LCMS *Handbook* states in Bylaw 5.2.3f that "He shall seek to strengthen the spirit of cooperation among pastors, commissioned ministers, and congregations."[21] Further, Bylaw 5.2.3.2 states that "The circuit visitor shall serve the pastors of the circuit as a collegial and brotherly advisor, reminding them of the joy of the ministry and of its great responsibilities"[22] while Bylaw 5.2.3.3 states that "The circuit visitor shall assist the district president, as assigned, in the ecclesiastical supervision of the other members of the Synod in the circuit."[23]

There is a missing element in this structure. Commissioned ministers, just like pastors, are in need of the support of a "collegial and brotherly advisor." This may often be done by their pastor or other commissioned ministers; however, the work of the circuit visitor to help ensure that all workers are cared for would go a long way toward the long-term health of church workers.

The primary locus of church worker care, however, is and will always be in the local congregation. Many churches do an excellent job observing clergy appreciation month in October. How many similarly include their other workers? Schools tend to have solid systems in place to provide for teacher appreciation gifts and/or events. Churches with congregationally based commissioned ministers should make sure to include their full ministry staff in some way in celebration of their ministry together. Anniversary celebrations for congregations should not only include noting the historic ministry of prior pastors, but if there are other called staff, they should not be omitted. District and congregational celebrations of milestones in ministry (years of service) should be as consistent as possible.

CONCLUSION

Why has all this been necessary? From my perspective, this issue speaks to the right relationship between pastors, commissioned ministers, and the

---

20 This is no simple ask. Districts with strong traditions for their educators and pastors conferences may struggle with the implementation of such an all-workers conference.

21 The Lutheran Church—Missouri Synod, *Handbook of The Lutheran Church—Missouri Synod,* 187.

22 The Lutheran Church—Missouri Synod, *Handbook,* 188.

23 The Lutheran Church—Missouri Synod, *Handbook,* 188.

churches and schools they serve. Being colleagues in ministry sets the relationship between the pastors and commissioned ministers as distinct and sacred. Recognizing the ministry of commissioned workers on the part of the churches and schools that call them impacts what is considered to be appropriate treatment of those workers. While we officially hold to an understanding that called workers are not to be simply hired and fired, our practice does not always reflect that official standard.

It is my hope that—having articulated the place of commissioned ministry as a part of the Office of Public Ministry—the common practice of referencing clergy and laity will be replaced with a fuller acknowledgment of the ministry of commissioned workers alongside pastors. Further, I hope that commissioned ministers themselves may come to better appreciate their own contribution to the ministry of the local church and school as well as the larger kingdom of God. Finally, I hope that there is a stronger sense of mutual respect shared among clergy, laity, and commissioned workers.

It is my prayer that articulation of a clearer theology of commissioned ministry that elevates both the pastoral office as well as commissioned ministers, while at the same time holding them in proper distinction from one another, will encourage a greater level of respect, collegiality, and shared ministry in our churches and schools locally, nationally, and internationally.

Appendix

The following charts represent data provided by the Office of Rosters and Statistics of the LCMS in January 10, 2019. Multiple methods are used to lay out the data to give as robust a picture as possible of the church workers in the LCMS.

Commissioned Ministers by Classification and District

ATLANTIC DISTRICT				
ACTIVE	53	DCE	Active	2
CANDIDATE	19	Deaconess	Active	3
EMERITUS	24	DPM	Active	1
Total:	96	Lay Minister	Active	1
		Teacher	Active	46
		Teacher	Candidate	19
		Teacher	Emeritus	24
Total:				**96**

CALIFORNIA-NEVADA-HAWAII DISTRICT				
ACTIVE	172	DCE	Active	22
CANDIDATE	39	Deaconess	Active	5
EMERITUS	62	DPM	Active	2
Total:	273	Lay Minister	Active	1
		Teach/DCE	Active	2
		Teacher	Active	140
		DCE	Candidate	8
		DCO	Candidate	1
		Teacher	Candidate	30
		DCE	Emeritus	1
		Deaconess	Emeritus	3
		Lay Minister	Emeritus	2
		Teach/DCE	Emeritus	4
		Teacher	Emeritus	52
Total:				**273**

CENTRAL ILLINOIS DISTRICT				
ACTIVE	182	DCE	Active	14
CANDIDATE	21	DPM	Active	1
EMERITUS	84	Lay Minister	Active	2
Total:	287	Parish Assistant	Active	1
		Teach/DCE	Active	4
		Teacher	Active	160
		DCE	Candidate	2
		Deaconess	Candidate	2

		Lay Minister	Candidate	1
		Teach/DCE	Candidate	1
		Teacher	Candidate	15
		Deaconess	Emeritus	1
		Teach/DCE	Emeritus	1
		Teacher	Emeritus	82
Total:				**287**

EASTERN DISTRICT

ACTIVE	43	DCE	Active	4
CANDIDATE	20	Deaconess	Active	3
EMERITUS	23	Teach/DCE	Active	4
Total:	86	Teacher	Active	32
		DCE	Candidate	1
		Deaconess	Candidate	1
		DFLM	Candidate	1
		Parish Assistant	Candidate	1
		Teach/DCE	Candidate	1
		Teacher	Candidate	15
		Deaconess	Emeritus	4
		Teach/DCE	Emeritus	1
		Teacher	Emeritus	18
Total:				**86**

ENGLISH DISTRICT

ACTIVE	62	DCE	Active	5
CANDIDATE	25	Deaconess	Active	5
EMERITUS	71	DFLM	Active	1
Total:	158	DPM	Active	3
		Lay Minister	Active	2
		Teach/DCE	Active	1
		Teacher	Active	45
		DCE	Candidate	5
		Deaconess	Candidate	2
		Teacher	Candidate	18
		DCE	Emeritus	1
		DCO	Emeritus	1
		Deaconess	Emeritus	1
		Lay Minister	Emeritus	5
		Teach/DCE	Emeritus	2
		Teacher	Emeritus	61
Total:				**158**

FLORIDA-GEORGIA DISTRICT

ACTIVE	174	DCE	Active	21
CANDIDATE	122	Deaconess	Active	11

EMERITUS	115	DFLM	Active	2
Total:	411	DPM	Active	1
		Teach/DCE	Active	3
		Teacher	Active	136
		DCE	Candidate	19
		Deaconess	Candidate	4
		Lay Minister	Candidate	1
		Teach/DCE	Candidate	2
		Teacher	Candidate	96
		DCE	Emeritus	4
		DCO	Emeritus	1
		Deaconess	Emeritus	1
		Lay Minister	Emeritus	3
		Parish Assistant	Emeritus	1
		Teach/DCE	Emeritus	4
		Teacher	Emeritus	101
Total:				**411**

INDIANA DISTRICT

ACTIVE	485	DCE	Active	27
CANDIDATE	104	Deaconess	Active	17
EMERITUS	268	DFLM	Active	1
Total:	857	DPM	Active	4
		Lay Minister	Active	2
		Teach/DCE	Active	7
		Teach/DPM	Active	1
		Teacher	Active	426
		DCE	Candidate	11
		Deaconess	Candidate	5
		Lay Minister	Candidate	1
		Teach/DCE	Candidate	1
		Teacher	Candidate	86
		DCE	Emeritus	1
		Deaconess	Emeritus	4
		Lay Minister	Emeritus	1
		Teach/DCE	Emeritus	6
		Teacher	Emeritus	256
Total:				**857**

IOWA EAST DISTRICT

ACTIVE	76	DCE	Active	6
CANDIDATE	22	Deaconess	Active	2
EMERITUS	30	Teach/DCE	Active	1
Total:	128	Teacher	Active	67
		DCE	Candidate	1

		DCO	Candidate	1
		Deaconess	Candidate	1
		Teach/DCE	Candidate	1
		Teacher	Candidate	18
		Teach/DCE	Emeritus	2
		Teacher	Emeritus	28
Total:				**128**

IOWA WEST DISTRICT				
ACTIVE	47	DCE	Active	10
CANDIDATE	29	DCO	Active	1
EMERITUS	26	Deaconess	Active	2
Total:	102	Lay Minister	Active	1
		Teach/DCE	Active	1
		Teacher	Active	32
		DCE	Candidate	5
		DPM	Candidate	1
		Teacher	Candidate	23
		DCE	Emeritus	1
		Deaconess	Emeritus	1
		Teach/DCE	Emeritus	1
		Teacher	Emeritus	23
Total:				**102**

KANSAS DISTRICT				
ACTIVE	86	DCE	Active	17
CANDIDATE	53	DPM	Active	1
EMERITUS	51	Teach/DCE	Active	5
Total:	190	Teacher	Active	63
		DCE	Candidate	11
		Deaconess	Candidate	1
		Lay Minister	Candidate	1
		Parish Assistant	Candidate	1
		Teach/DCE	Candidate	3
		Teacher	Candidate	36
		DCE	Emeritus	1
		Deaconess	Emeritus	1
		Teach/DCE	Emeritus	6
		Teacher	Emeritus	43
Total:				**190**

MICHIGAN DISTRICT				
ACTIVE	562	DCE	Active	26
CANDIDATE	75	DCO	Active	2
EMERITUS	407	Deaconess	Active	8
Total:	1,044	DFLM	Active	23

		DPM	Active	8
		Lay Minister	Active	2
		Parish Assistant	Active	4
		Teach/DCE	Active	17
		Teach/DCE/DCO	Active	1
		Teacher	Active	471
		DCE	Candidate	6
		Deaconess	Candidate	1
		DFLM	Candidate	4
		Teach/DCE	Candidate	1
		Teacher	Candidate	63
		DCE	Emeritus	3
		Deaconess	Emeritus	6
		Lay Minister	Emeritus	4
		Parish Assistant	Emeritus	2
		Teach/DCE	Emeritus	5
		Teacher	Emeritus	387
Total:				**1,044**

MID-SOUTH DISTRICT

ACTIVE	53	DCE	Active	7
CANDIDATE	14	Deaconess	Active	1
EMERITUS	37	DFLM	Active	1
Total:	104	DPM	Active	4
		Teach/DCE	Active	2
		Teacher	Active	38
		DCO	Candidate	1
		Teacher	Candidate	13
		Teacher	Emeritus	37
Total:				**104**

MINNESOTA NORTH DISTRICT

ACTIVE	41	DCE	Active	9
CANDIDATE	22	DCO	Active	1
EMERITUS	26	Deaconess	Active	2
Total:	89	Lay Minister	Active	1
		Teach/DCE	Active	1
		Teacher	Active	27
		DCE	Candidate	3
		DCO	Candidate	2
		Deaconess	Candidate	2
		Teach/DCE	Candidate	1
		Teacher	Candidate	14
		DCE	Emeritus	1
		DCO	Emeritus	2

		Deaconess	Emeritus	1
		Teach/DCE	Emeritus	1
		Teacher	Emeritus	21
Total:				**89**

MINNESOTA SOUTH DISTRICT

ACTIVE	311	DCE	Active	40
CANDIDATE	103	DCO	Active	4
EMERITUS	175	Deaconess	Active	4
Total:	589	DFLM	Active	1
		DPM	Active	4
		Lay Minister	Active	2
		Teach/DCE	Active	7
		Teacher	Active	249
		DCE	Candidate	16
		DCO	Candidate	5
		Deaconess	Candidate	3
		Lay Minister	Candidate	4
		Teach/DCE	Candidate	2
		Teacher	Candidate	73
		DCE	Emeritus	2
		DCO	Emeritus	2
		Deaconess	Emeritus	4
		Lay Minister	Emeritus	1
		Teach/DCE	Emeritus	6
		Teacher	Emeritus	160
Total:				**589**

MISSOURI DISTRICT

ACTIVE	581	DCE	Active	36
CANDIDATE	95	DCO	Active	1
EMERITUS	311	Deaconess	Active	28
Total:	987	DFLM	Active	1
		DPM	Active	8
		Lay Minister	Active	7
		Teach/DCE	Active	8
		Teacher	Active	492
		DCE	Candidate	11
		DCO	Candidate	1
		Deaconess	Candidate	6
		DPM	Candidate	2
		Teach/DCE	Candidate	5
		Teacher	Candidate	70
		DCE	Emeritus	4
		DCO	Emeritus	1

		Deaconess	Emeritus	2
		Lay Minister	Emeritus	1
		Teach/DCE	Emeritus	4
		Teach/DCE/DCO	Emeritus	1
		Teacher	Emeritus	298
Total:				**987**

MONTANA DISTRICT

ACTIVE	19	Deaconess	Active	1
CANDIDATE	6	DPM	Active	1
EMERITUS	13	Lay Minister	Active	1
Total:	38	Teacher	Active	16
		DCE	Candidate	1
		Deaconess	Candidate	1
		Teacher	Candidate	4
		Lay Minister	Emeritus	1
		Teacher	Emeritus	12
Total:				**38**

NEBRASKA DISTRICT

ACTIVE	320	DCE	Active	23
CANDIDATE	108	DCO	Active	1
EMERITUS	175	Deaconess	Active	6
Total:	603	DFLM	Active	2
		DPM	Active	3
		Lay Minister	Active	3
		Teach/DCE	Active	9
		Teacher	Active	273
		DCE	Candidate	5
		DPM	Candidate	1
		Lay Minister	Candidate	1
		Teach/DCE	Candidate	1
		Teacher	Candidate	100
		DCE	Emeritus	1
		DPM	Emeritus	1
		Teach/DCE	Emeritus	2
		Teacher	Emeritus	171
Total:				**603**

NEW ENGLAND DISTRICT

ACTIVE	14	Deaconess	Active	4
CANDIDATE	13	Lay Minister	Active	2
EMERITUS	16	Teacher	Active	8
Total:	43	DCE	Candidate	3
		Deaconess	Candidate	1
		Lay Minister	Candidate	1

		Position	Status	Count
		Parish Assistant	Candidate	1
		Teacher	Candidate	7
		Deaconess	Emeritus	1
		Teacher	Emeritus	15
Total:				**43**

NEW JERSEY DISTRICT

ACTIVE	3	DCE	Active	1
CANDIDATE	11	Teacher	Active	2
EMERITUS	8	DCE	Candidate	2
Total:	22	Teacher	Candidate	9
		Deaconess	Emeritus	1
		Lay Minister	Emeritus	1
		Teacher	Emeritus	6
Total:				**22**

NORTH DAKOTA DISTRICT

ACTIVE	17	DCE	Active	4
CANDIDATE	11	Deaconess	Active	3
EMERITUS	1	Teacher	Active	10
Total:	29	DCE	Candidate	1
		DPM	Candidate	1
		Teach/DCE	Candidate	1
		Teacher	Candidate	8
		Teacher	Emeritus	1
Total:				**29**

NORTH WISCONSIN DISTRICT

ACTIVE	190	DCE	Active	19
CANDIDATE	28	DCO	Active	1
EMERITUS	66	Deaconess	Active	2
Total:	284	DPM	Active	3
		Lay Minister	Active	11
		Teach/DCE	Active	3
		Teach/DPM	Active	1
		Teacher	Active	150
		DCE	Candidate	4
		DCO	Candidate	2
		Deaconess	Candidate	2
		Lay Minister	Candidate	2
		Teach/DCE	Candidate	1
		Teacher	Candidate	17
		DCE	Emeritus	1
		Deaconess	Emeritus	2
		Lay Minister	Emeritus	3
		Teacher	Emeritus	60

Total:				284

NORTHERN ILLINOIS DISTRICT

ACTIVE	545	DCE	Active	25
CANDIDATE	164	DCO	Active	2
EMERITUS	270	Deaconess	Active	20
Total:	979	DFLM	Active	1
		DPM	Active	4
		Lay Minister	Active	16
		Teach/DCE	Active	6
		Teacher	Active	471
		DCE	Candidate	14
		DCO	Candidate	2
		Deaconess	Candidate	11
		DFLM	Candidate	1
		Lay Minister	Candidate	3
		Teach/DCE	Candidate	5
		Teacher	Candidate	128
		DCE	Emeritus	1
		Deaconess	Emeritus	3
		Lay Minister	Emeritus	1
		Teach/DCE	Emeritus	2
		Teacher	Emeritus	263
Total:				**979**

NORTHWEST DISTRICT

ACTIVE	184	DCE	Active	29
CANDIDATE	82	Deaconess	Active	8
EMERITUS	124	DFLM	Active	2
Total:	390	DPM	Active	1
		Teach/DCE	Active	4
		Teach/DPM	Active	1
		Teacher	Active	139
		DCE	Candidate	19
		Deaconess	Candidate	1
		Teach/DCE	Candidate	4
		Teacher	Candidate	58
		DCE	Emeritus	4
		Deaconess	Emeritus	2
		Lay Minister	Emeritus	1
		Teach/DCE	Emeritus	3
		Teacher	Emeritus	114
Total:				**390**

OHIO DISTRICT

ACTIVE	124	DCE	Active	11

CANDIDATE	32	Deaconess	Active	4
EMERITUS	67	DFLM	Active	4
Total:	223	Teach/DCE	Active	2
		Teacher	Active	103
		DCE	Candidate	2
		DCO	Candidate	1
		Deaconess	Candidate	3
		Teacher	Candidate	26
		Deaconess	Emeritus	1
		Lay Minister	Emeritus	1
		Teach/DCE	Emeritus	2
		Teacher	Emeritus	63
Total:				**223**

OKLAHOMA DISTRICT

ACTIVE	52	DCE	Active	7
CANDIDATE	17	Deaconess	Active	2
EMERITUS	15	Lay Minister	Active	5
Total:	84	Parish Assistant	Active	2
		Teach/DCE	Active	2
		Teach/DPM	Active	1
		Teacher	Active	33
		DCE	Candidate	4
		Deaconess	Candidate	2
		DPM	Candidate	1
		Parish Assistant	Candidate	1
		Teacher	Candidate	9
		Teach/DCE	Emeritus	1
		Teacher	Emeritus	14
Total:				**84**

PACIFIC SOUTHWEST DISTRICT

ACTIVE	627	DCE	Active	62
CANDIDATE	155	Deaconess	Active	6
EMERITUS	245	DPM	Active	7
Total:	1,027	Lay Minister	Active	2
		Teach/DCE	Active	10
		Teacher	Active	540
		DCE	Candidate	15
		DCO	Candidate	2
		DFLM	Candidate	1
		DPM	Candidate	1
		Teach/DCE	Candidate	3
		Teacher	Candidate	133
		DCE	Emeritus	4

		Deaconess	Emeritus	5
		Lay Minister	Emeritus	2
		Teach/DCE	Emeritus	8
		Teacher	Emeritus	226
Total:				**1,027**

ROCKY MOUNTAIN DISTRICT

ACTIVE	194	DCE	Active	19
CANDIDATE	116	DCO	Active	1
EMERITUS	100	Deaconess	Active	2
Total:	410	DFLM	Active	1
		DPM	Active	4
		Teach/DCE	Active	4
		Teacher	Active	163
		DCE	Candidate	9
		Deaconess	Candidate	3
		DPM	Candidate	1
		Lay Minister	Candidate	1
		Teach/DCE	Candidate	2
		Teacher	Candidate	100
		DCE	Emeritus	3
		DCO	Emeritus	2
		Deaconess	Emeritus	2
		Lay Minister	Emeritus	1
		Teach/DCE	Emeritus	5
		Teacher	Emeritus	87
Total:				**410**

SELC DISTRICT

ACTIVE	23	DCE	Active	3
CANDIDATE	10	Deaconess	Active	1
EMERITUS	7	DFLM	Active	1
Total:	40	Teacher	Active	18
		DCE	Candidate	1
		Deaconess	Candidate	1
		Teacher	Candidate	8
		Teacher	Emeritus	7
Total:				**40**

SOUTH DAKOTA DISTRICT

ACTIVE	33	DCE	Active	6
CANDIDATE	16	Teacher	Active	27
EMERITUS	14	DCE	Candidate	3
Total:	63	Deaconess	Candidate	3
		Teacher	Candidate	10
		Lay Minister	Emeritus	1

		Teacher	Emeritus	13
Total:				**63**

SOUTH WISCONSIN DISTRICT

ACTIVE	640	DCE	Active	10
CANDIDATE	69	Deaconess	Active	10
EMERITUS	216	DPM	Active	6
Total:	925	Lay Minister	Active	5
		Parish Assistant	Active	1
		Teach/DCE	Active	5
		Teach/DCE/DCO	Active	1
		Teacher	Active	602
		DCE	Candidate	8
		Deaconess	Candidate	3
		Lay Minister	Candidate	5
		Teacher	Candidate	53
		DCE	Emeritus	1
		Deaconess	Emeritus	5
		Lay Minister	Emeritus	4
		Teach/DCE	Emeritus	1
		Teacher	Emeritus	205
Total:				**925**

SOUTHEASTERN DISTRICT

ACTIVE	139	DCE	Active	25
CANDIDATE	52	DCO	Active	1
EMERITUS	79	Deaconess	Active	6
Total:	270	DPM	Active	2
		Lay Minister	Active	9
		Teach/DCE	Active	2
		Teacher	Active	94
		DCE	Candidate	6
		DFLM	Candidate	1
		Lay Minister	Candidate	2
		Teach/DCE	Candidate	2
		Teacher	Candidate	41
		DCE	Emeritus	1
		DCO	Emeritus	1
		Deaconess	Emeritus	2
		Lay Minister	Emeritus	2
		Teacher	Emeritus	73
Total:				**270**

SOUTHERN DISTRICT

ACTIVE	39	DCE	Active	6
CANDIDATE	26	Deaconess	Active	2

EMERITUS	40	DPM	Active	1
Total:	105	Teach/DCE	Active	2
		Teacher	Active	28
		DCE	Candidate	3
		DCO	Candidate	1
		Deaconess	Candidate	2
		Teach/DCE	Candidate	1
		Teacher	Candidate	19
		Deaconess	Emeritus	3
		Lay Minister	Emeritus	1
		Teach/DCE	Emeritus	2
		Teacher	Emeritus	34
Total:				**105**

SOUTHERN ILLINOIS DISTRICT

ACTIVE	148	DCE	Active	4
CANDIDATE	35	Deaconess	Active	2
EMERITUS	72	DPM	Active	1
Total:	255	Teach/DCE	Active	2
		Teacher	Active	139
		DCE	Candidate	2
		Deaconess	Candidate	1
		Teach/DCE	Candidate	2
		Teacher	Candidate	30
		Deaconess	Emeritus	1
		Lay Minister	Emeritus	1
		Teacher	Emeritus	70
Total:				**255**

TEXAS DISTRICT

ACTIVE	633	DCE	Active	91
CANDIDATE	112	DCO	Active	2
EMERITUS	220	Deaconess	Active	10
Total:	965	DFLM	Active	1
		DPM	Active	6
		Lay Minister	Active	4
		Teach/DCE	Active	6
		Teacher	Active	513
		DCE	Candidate	21
		Deaconess	Candidate	4
		Teach/DCE	Candidate	2
		Teacher	Candidate	85
		Deaconess	Emeritus	3
		Lay Minister	Emeritus	7
		Teach/DCE	Emeritus	13

		Teacher	Emeritus	197
Total:				**965**
WYOMING DISTRICT				
ACTIVE	8	Teacher	Active	8
CANDIDATE	11	DCE	Candidate	2
EMERITUS	5	Teacher	Candidate	9
Total:	24	Teacher	Emeritus	5
		Total:		24
			GRAND TOTAL:	**12,180**

ACTIVE COMMISSIONED MINISTERS BY CLASSIFICATION AND DISTRICT

DISTRICT	ALL	DCE	DCO	DCS	DFLM	DPM	LAY MIN	PAR. ASST.	TEACHER	TEACH/ DCE	TEACH/ DCE/DCO	TEACH/ DPM
Atlantic	53	2	0	3	0	1	1	0	46	0	0	0
CA/NV/HI	172	22	0	5	0	2	1	0	140	2	0	0
Central Illinois	182	14	0	0	0	1	2	1	160	4	0	0
Eastern	43	4	0	3	0	0	0	0	32	4	0	0
English	62	5	0	5	1	3	2	0	45	1	0	0
Florida/Georgia	174	21	0	11	2	1	0	0	136	3	0	0
Indiana	485	27	0	17	1	4	2	0	426	7	0	1
Iowa East	76	6	0	2	0	0	0	0	67	1	0	0
Iowa West	47	10	1	2	0	0	1	0	32	1	0	0
Kansas	86	17	0	0	0	1	0	0	63	5	0	0
Michigan	562	26	2	8	23	8	2	4	471	17	1	0
Mid-South	53	7	0	1	1	4	0	0	38	2	0	0
Minnesota North	41	9	1	2	0	0	1	0	27	1	0	0
Minnesota South	311	40	4	4	1	4	2	0	249	7	0	0
Missouri	581	36	1	28	1	8	7	0	492	8	0	0
Montana	19	0	0	1	0	1	1	0	16	0	0	0
Nebraska	323	23	1	6	2	3	3	0	273	9	0	0
New England	14	0	0	4	0	0	2	0	8	0	0	0
New Jersey	3	1	0	0	0	0	0	0	2	0	0	0
North Dakota	17	4	0	3	0	0	0	0	10	0	0	0
North Wisconsin	190	19	1	2	0	3	11	0	150	3	0	1
Northern Illinois	545	25	2	20	1	4	16	0	471	6	0	0
Northwest	184	29	0	8	2	1	0	0	139	4	0	1
Ohio	124	11	0	4	4	0	0	0	103	2	0	0
Oklahoma	52	7	0	2	0	0	5	2	33	2	0	1
Pacific Southwest	627	62	0	6	0	7	2	0	540	10	0	0
Rocky Mountain	194	19	1	2	1	4	0	0	163	4	0	0
SELC	23	3	0	1	1	0	0	0	18	0	0	0
South Dakota	33	6	0	0	0	0	0	0	27	0	0	0
South Wisconsin	640	10	0	10	0	6	5	1	602	5	1	0
Southeastern	139	25	1	6	0	2	9	0	94	2	0	0
Southern	39	6	0	2	0	1	0	0	28	2	0	0
Southern Illinois	148	4	0	2	0	1	0	0	139	2	0	0
Texas	633	91	2	10	1	6	4	0	513	6	0	0
Wyoming	8	0	0	0	0	0	0	0	8	0	0	0
Totals	**6883**	**591**	**17**	**180**	**42**	**76**	**79**	**8**	**5761**	**120**	**2**	**4**

CANDIDATE COMMISSIONED MINISTERS BY CLASSIFICATION AND DISTRICT

DISTRICT	ALL	DCE	DCO	DCS	DFLM	DPM	LAY MIN	PAR. AST.	TEACHER	TEACH/ DCE
Atlantic	19	0	0	0	0	0	0	0	19	0
CA/NV/HI	39	8	1	0	0	0	0	0	30	0
Central Illinois	21	2	0	2	0	0	1	0	15	1
Eastern	20	1	0	1	1	0	0	1	15	1
English	25	5	0	2	0	0	0	0	18	0
Florida/Georgia	122	19	0	4	0	0	1	0	96	2
Indiana	104	11	0	5	0	0	1	0	86	1
Iowa East	22	1	1	1	0	0	0	0	18	1
Iowa West	29	5	0	0	0	1	0	0	23	0
Kansas	53	11	0	1	0	0	1	1	36	3
Michigan	75	6	0	1	4	0	0	0	63	1
Mid-South	14	0	1	0	0	0	0	0	13	1
Minnesota North	22	3	2	2	0	0	0	0	14	1
Minnesota South	103	16	5	3	0	0	4	0	73	2
Missouri	95	11	1	6	0	2	0	0	70	5
Montana	6	1	0	1	0	0	0	0	4	0
Nebraska	108	5	0	0	0	1	1	0	100	1
New England	13	3	0	1	0	0	1	1	7	0
New Jersey	11	2	0	0	0	0	0	0	9	0
North Dakota	11	1	0	0	0	1	0	0	8	1
North Wisconsin	28	4	2	2	0	0	2	0	17	1
Northern Illinois	164	14	2	11	1	0	3	0	128	5
Northwest	82	19	0	1	0	0	0	0	58	4
Ohio	32	2	1	3	0	0	0	0	26	0
Oklahoma	17	4	0	2	0	1	0	1	9	0
Pacific Southwest	155	15	2	0	1	1	0	0	133	3
Rocky Mountain	116	9	0	3	0	1	1	0	100	2
SELC	10	1	0	1	0	0	0	0	8	0
South Dakota	16	3	0	3	0	0	0	0	10	0
South Wisconsin	69	8	0	3	0	0	5	0	53	0
Southeastern	52	6	0	0	1	0	1	0	41	2
Southern	26	3	1	2	0	0	0	0	19	1
Southern Illinois	35	2	0	1	0	0	0	0	30	2
Texas	112	21	0	4	0	0	0	0	85	2
Wyoming	11	2	0	0	0	0	0	0	9	0
Totals	**1837**	**224**	**19**	**66**	**8**	**8**	**22**	**4**	**1443**	**43**

DISTRICT	ALL	DCE	DCO	DCS	DPM	LAY MIN	PAR. AST.	TEACHER	TEACH/DCE	TEACH/DCE
Atlantic	24	0	0	0	0	0	0	24	0	0
CA/NV/HI	62	1	0	3	0	2	0	52	4	0
Central Illinois	84	0	0	1	0	0	0	82	1	0
Eastern	23	0	0	4	0	0	0	18	1	0
English	71	1	1	1	0	5	0	61	2	0
Florida/Georgia	115	4	1	1	0	3	1	101	4	0
Indiana	268	1	0	4	0	1	0	256	6	0
Iowa East	30	0	0	0	0	0	0	28	2	0
Iowa West	26	1	0	1	0	0	0	23	1	0
Kansas	51	1	0	1	0	0	0	43	6	0
Michigan	407	3	0	6	0	4	2	387	5	0
Mid-South	37	0	0	0	0	0	0	37	0	0
Minnesota North	26	1	2	1	0	0	0	21	1	0
Minnesota South	175	2	2	4	0	1	0	160	6	0
Missouri	311	4	1	2	0	1	0	298	4	1
Montana	13	0	0	0	0	1	0	12	0	0
Nebraska	175	1	0	0	1	0	0	171	2	0
New England	16	0	0	1	0	0	0	15	0	0
New Jersey	8	0	0	1	0	1	0	6	0	0
North Dakota	1	0	0	0	0	0	0	1	0	0
North Wisconsin	66	1	0	2	0	3	0	60	0	0
Northern Illinois	270	1	0	3	0	1	0	263	2	0
Northwest	124	4	0	2	0	1	0	114	3	0
Ohio	67	0	0	1	0	1	0	63	2	0
Oklahoma	15	0	0	0	0	0	0	14	1	0
Pacific Southwest	245	4	0	5	0	2	0	226	8	0
Rocky Mountain	100	3	2	2	0	1	0	87	5	0
SELC	7	0	0	0	0	0	0	7	0	0
South Dakota	14	0	0	0	0	1	0	13	0	0
South Wisconsin	216	1	0	5	0	4	0	205	1	0
Southeastern	79	1	1	2	0	2	0	73	0	0
Southern	40	0	0	3	0	1	0	34	2	0
Southern Illinois	72	0	0	1	0	1	0	70	0	0
Texas	220	0	0	3	0	7	0	197	13	0
Wyoming	5	0	0	0	0	0	0	5	0	0
Totals	**3463**	**35**	**10**	**60**	**1**	**44**	**3**	**3227**	**82**	**1**

	ACTIVE		CANDIDATE		EMERITUS	
DISTRICT	**ORDAINED**	**COMMISSIONED**	**ORDAINED**	**COMMISSIONED**	**ORDAINED**	**COMMISSIONED**
Atlantic	99	53	4	19	34	24
California/Nevada/ Hawaii	165	172	18	39	114	62
Central Illinois	138	182	12	21	58	84
Eastern	107	43	8	20	56	23
English	174	62	9	25	87	71
Florida/Georgia	206	174	18	122	180	115
Indiana	307	485	24	104	168	268
Iowa East	103	76	5	22	37	30
Iowa West	144	47	2	29	51	26
Kansas	140	86	1	53	70	51
Michigan	397	562	14	75	203	407
Mid-South	119	53	9	14	65	37
Minnesota North	147	41	8	22	76	26
Minnesota South	256	311	15	103	142	175
Missouri	443	581	19	95	194	311
Montana	52	19	2	6	20	13
Nebraska	230	323	16	108	90	175
New England	64	14	4	13	33	16
New Jersey	43	3	7	11	25	8
North Dakota	53	17	4	11	11	1
North Wisconsin	173	190	8	28	96	66
Northern Illinois	254	545	11	164	114	270
Northwest	225	184	23	82	188	124
Ohio	153	124	5	32	88	67
Oklahoma	63	52	6	17	28	15
Pacific Southwest	333	627	33	155	184	245
Rocky Mountain	166	194	18	116	96	100
SELC	57	23	4	10	25	7
South Dakota	79	33	6	16	41	14
South Wisconsin	248	640	14	69	136	216
Southeastern	201	139	31	52	159	79
Southern	138	39	6	26	66	40
Southern Illinois	95	148	5	35	28	72
Texas	432	633	31	112	217	220
Wyoming	52	8	1	11	26	5
Totals	**6056**	**6883**	**401**	**1837**	**3463**	**3463**

BREAKDOWN OF ACTIVE COMMISSIONED MINISTERS BY CLASSIFICATIONS BY DISTRICT

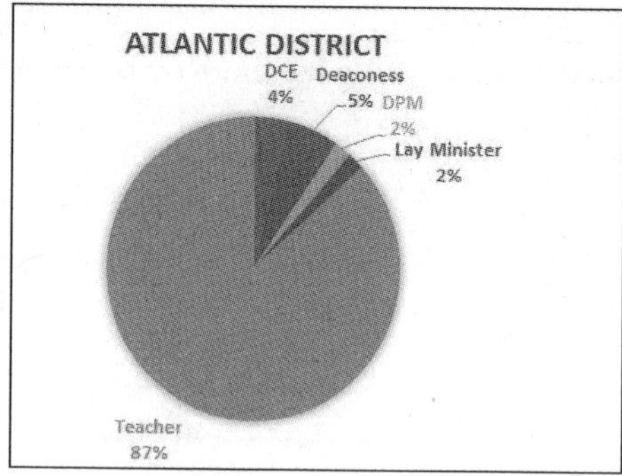

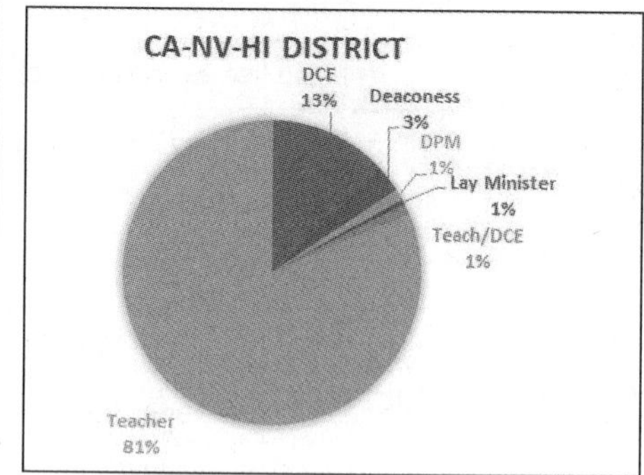

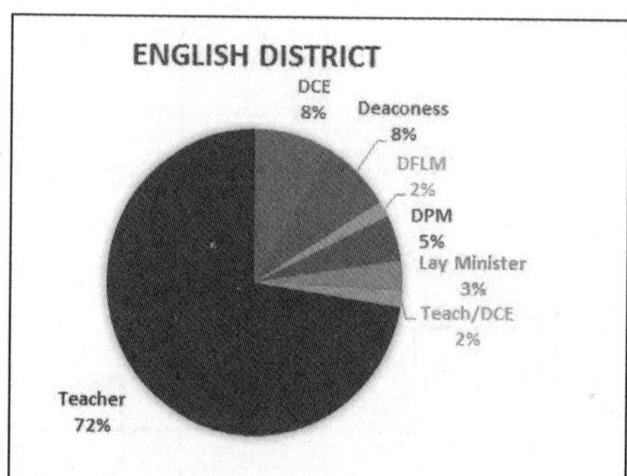

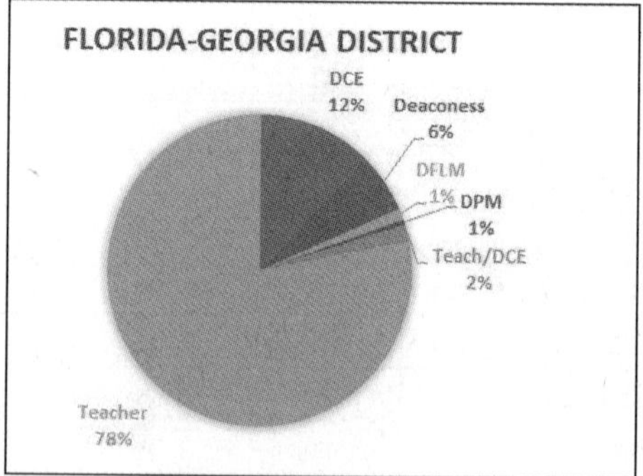

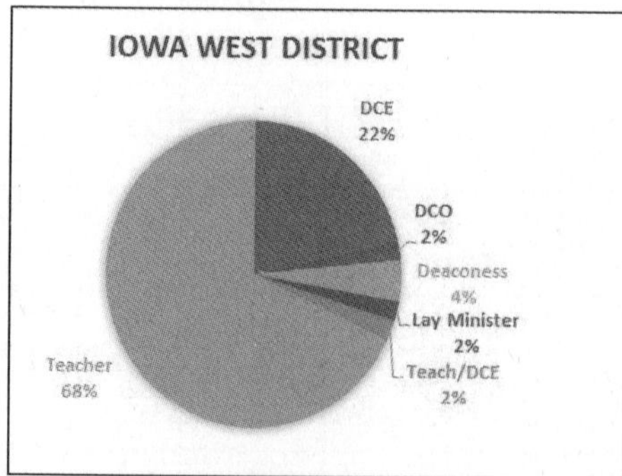

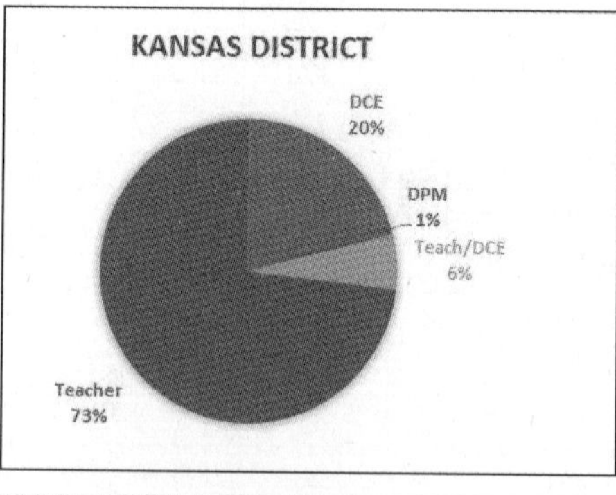

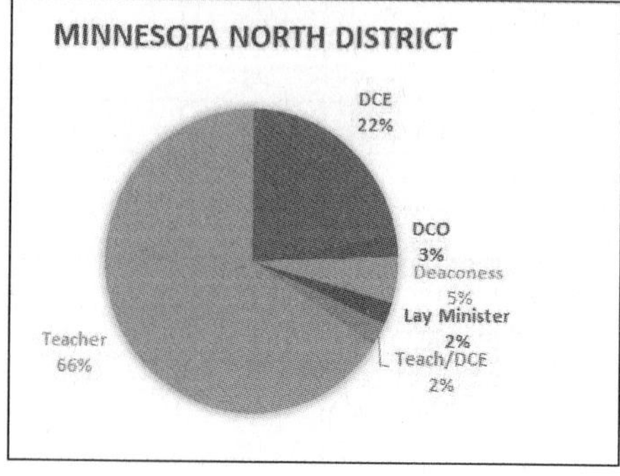

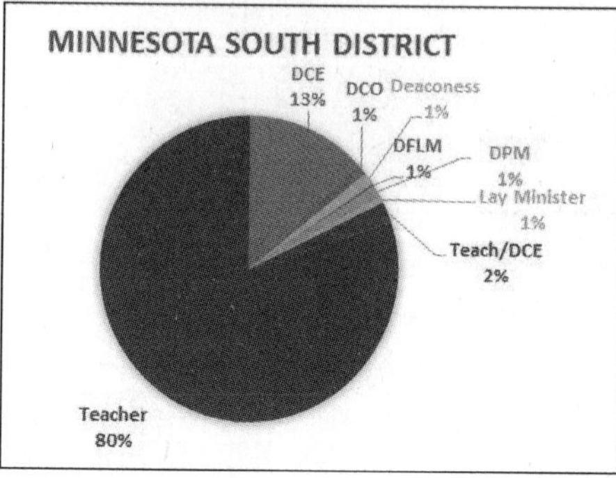

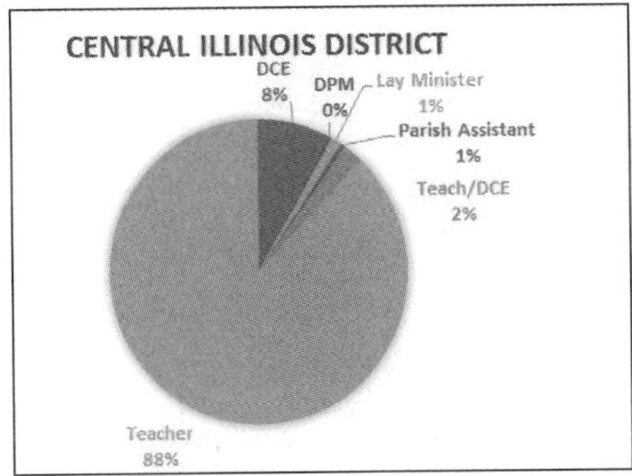

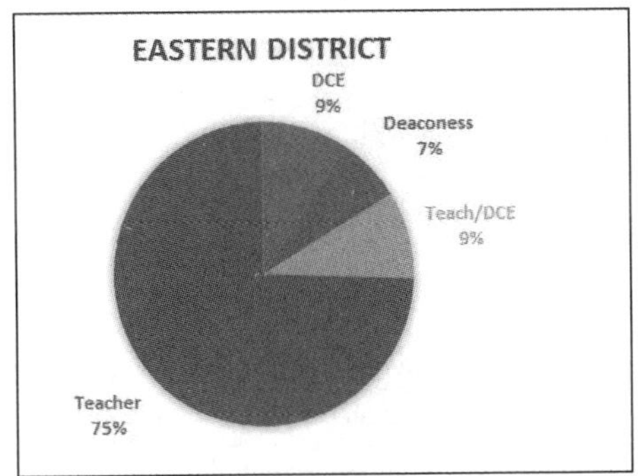

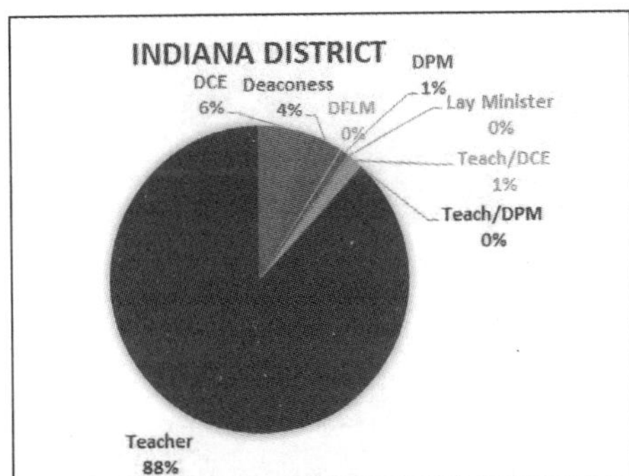

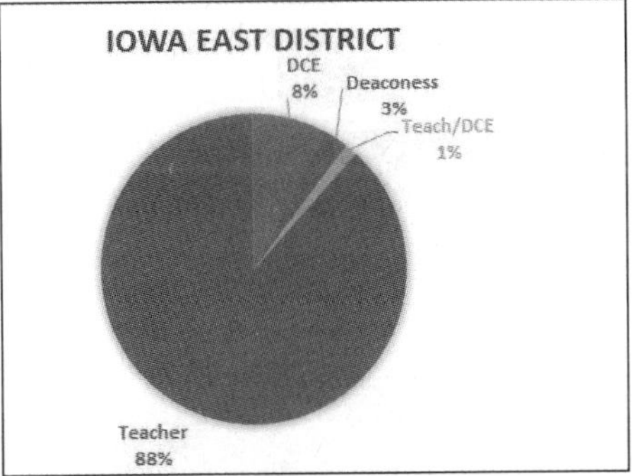

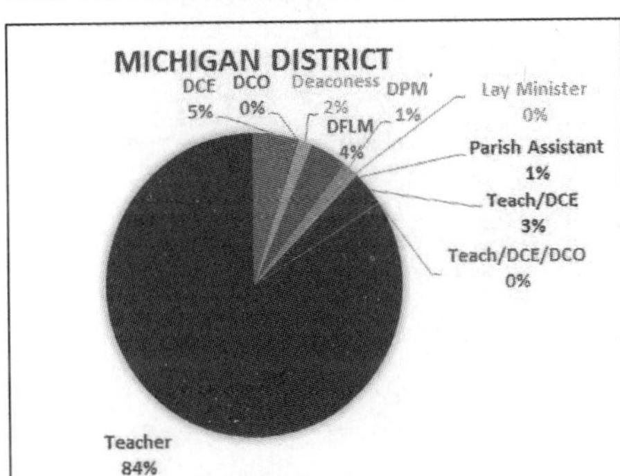

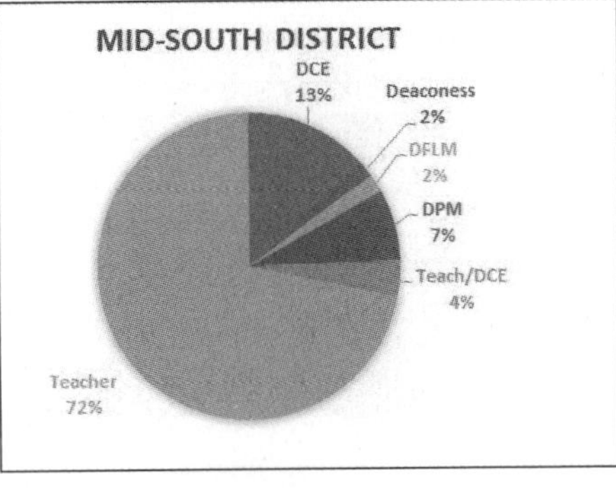

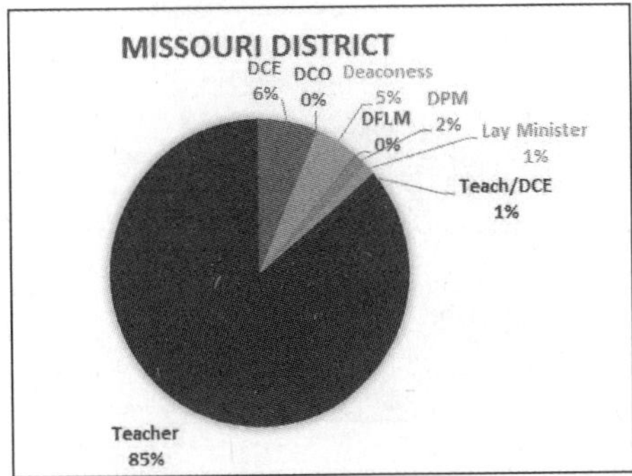

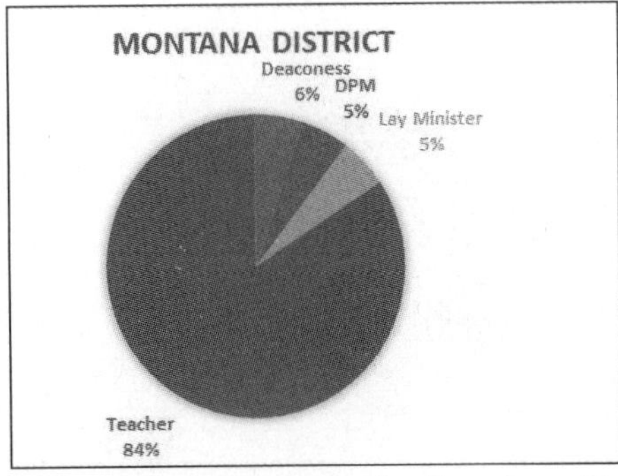

*Figures below 1% may be listed as 0%.

BREAKDOWN OF ACTIVE COMMISSIONED MINISTERS BY CLASSIFICATIONS BY DISTRICT

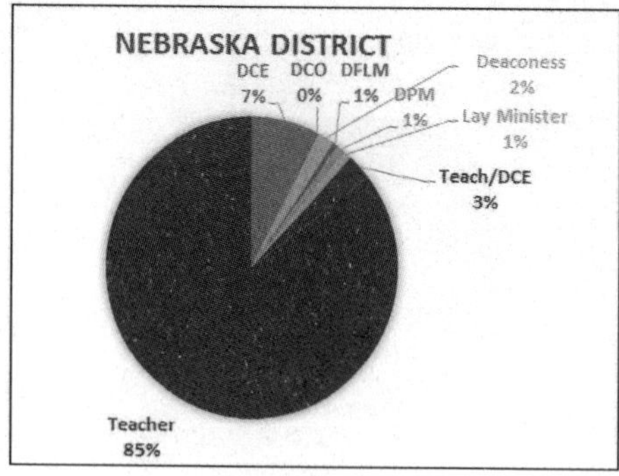

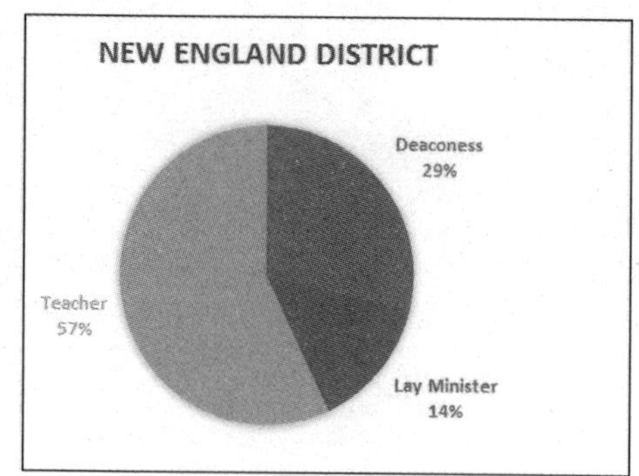

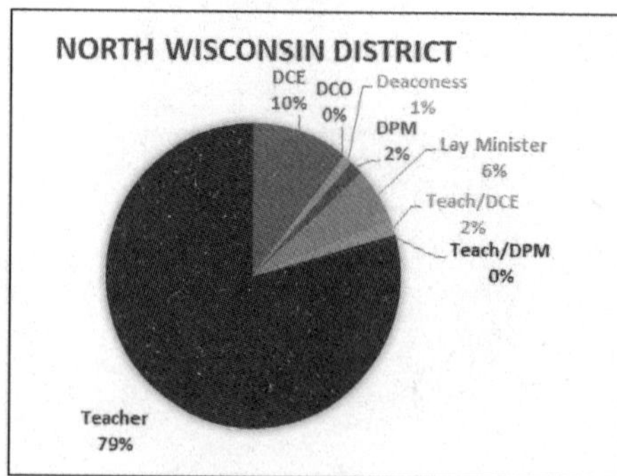

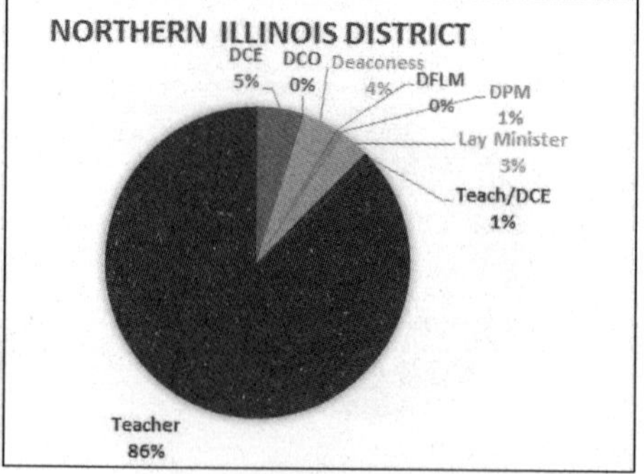

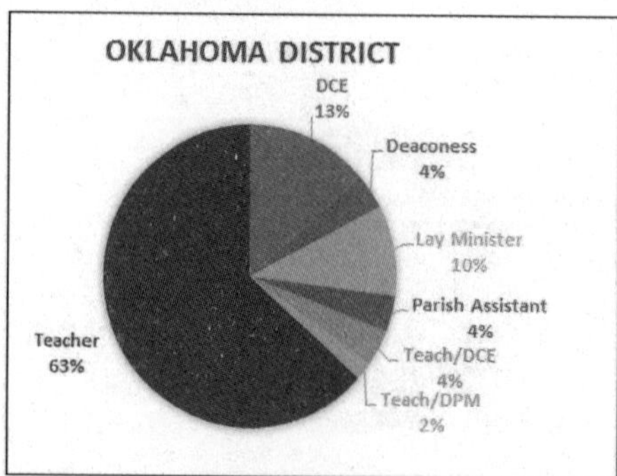

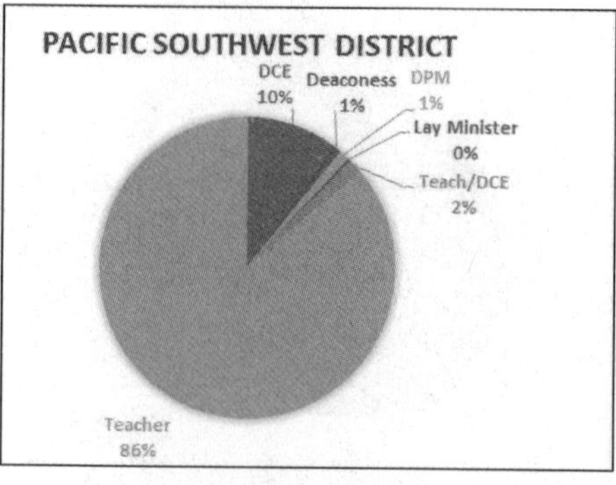

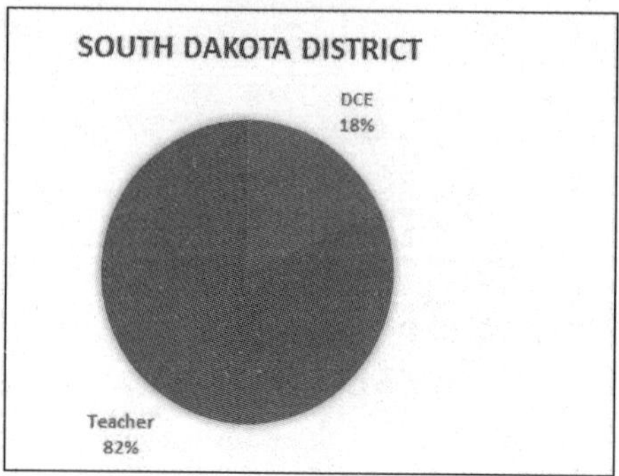

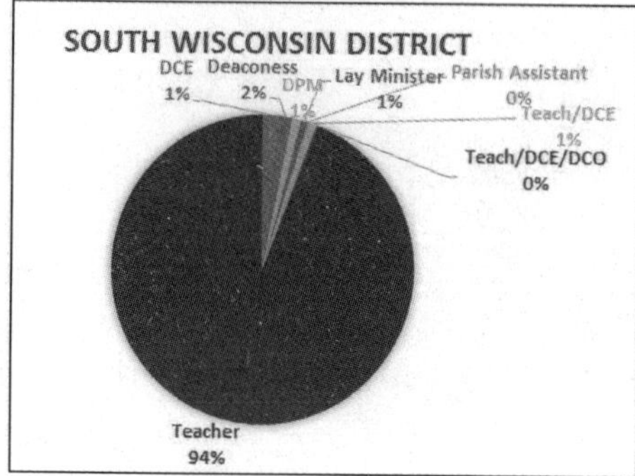

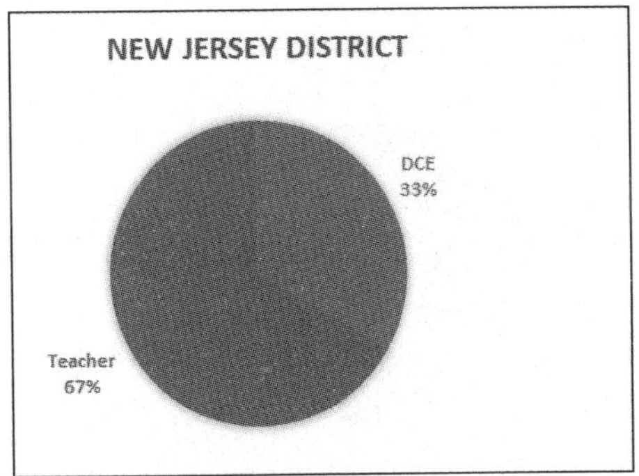

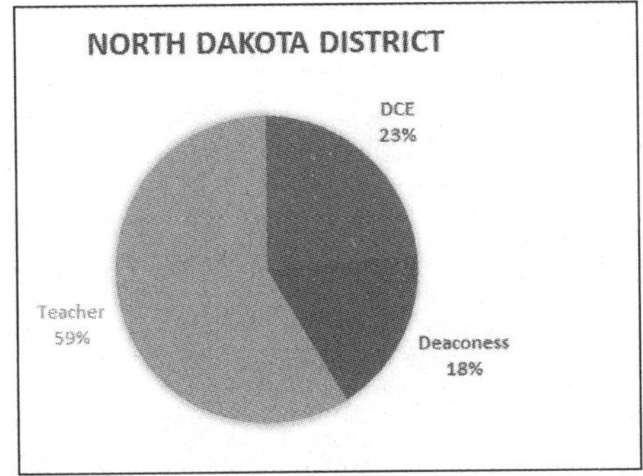

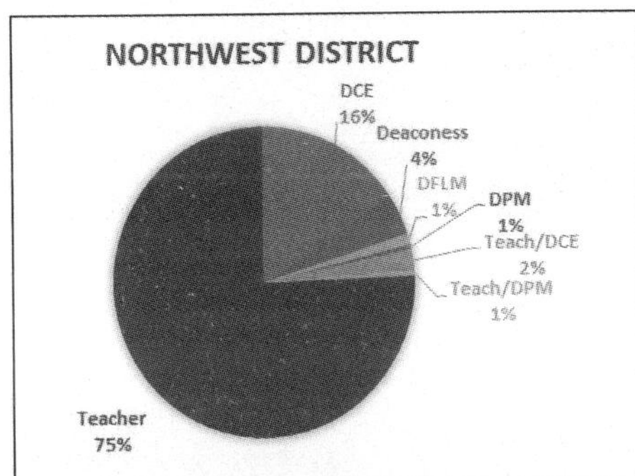

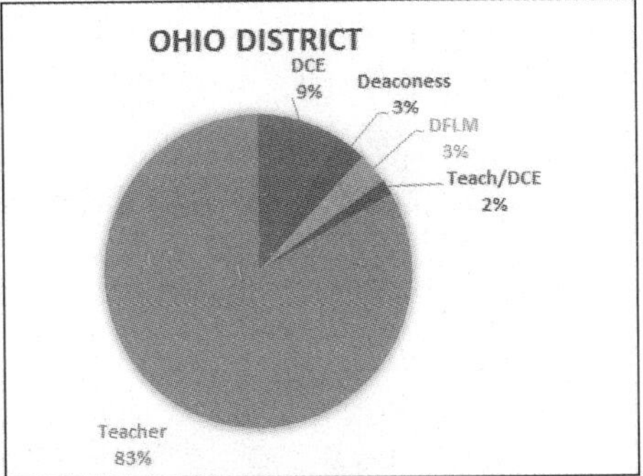

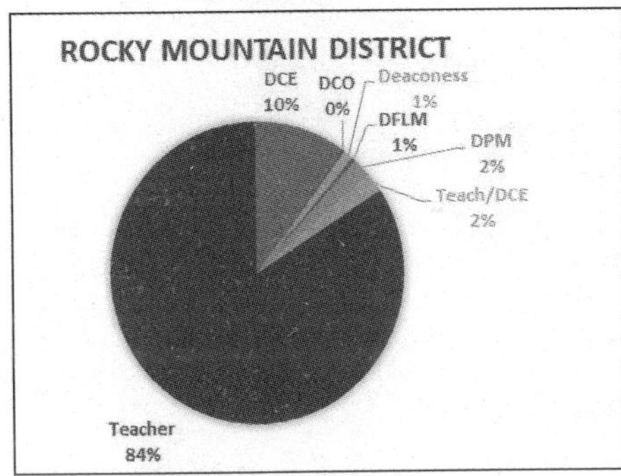

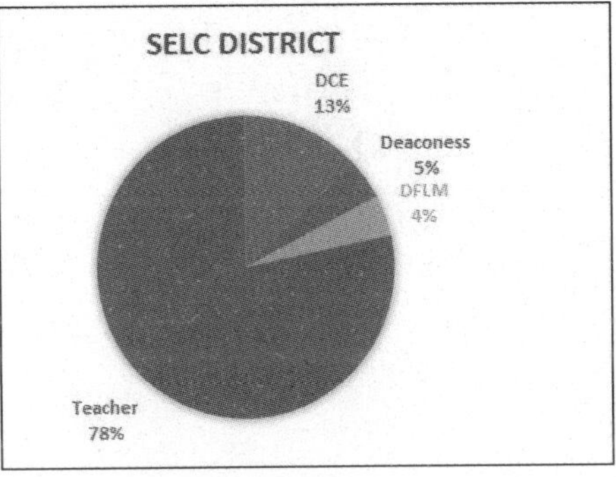

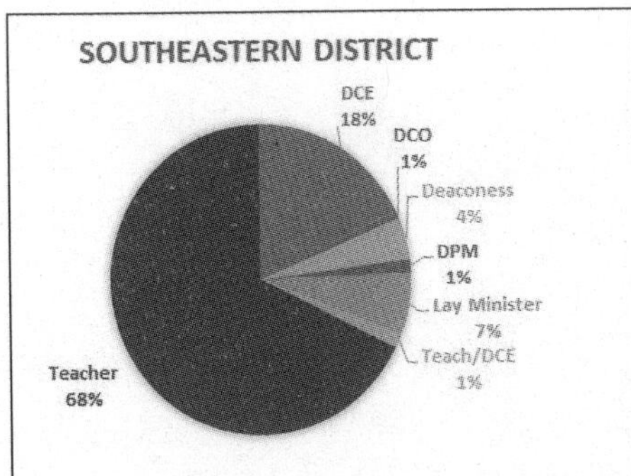

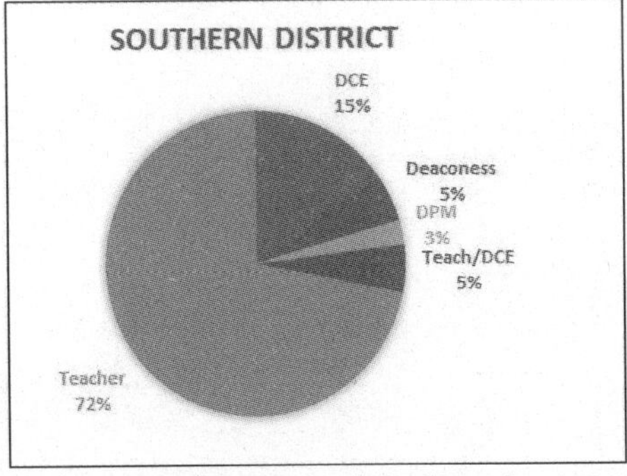

*Figures below 1% may be listed as 0%.

BREAKDOWN OF ACTIVE COMMISSIONED MINISTERS BY CLASSIFICATIONS BY DISTRICT

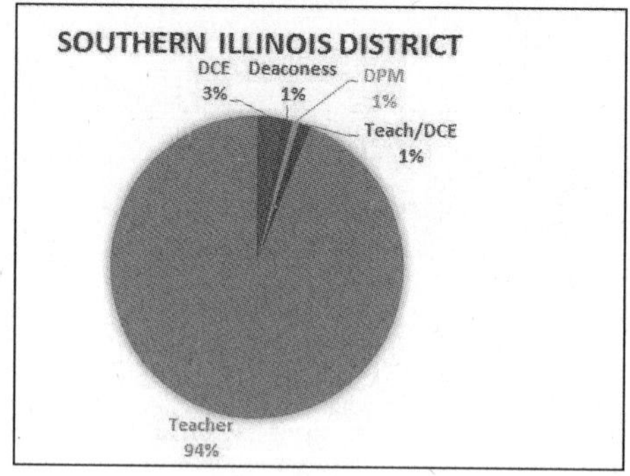

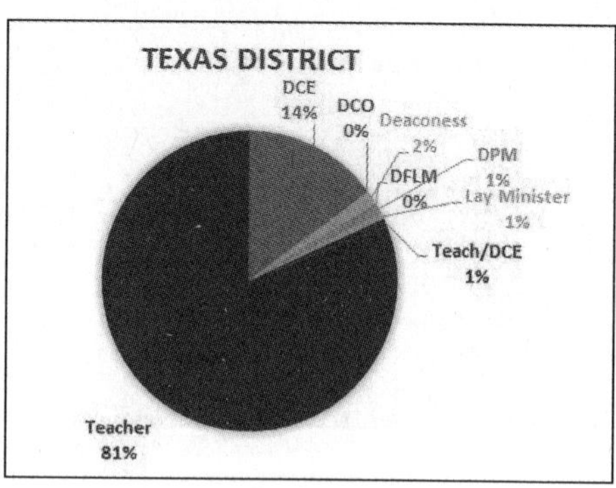

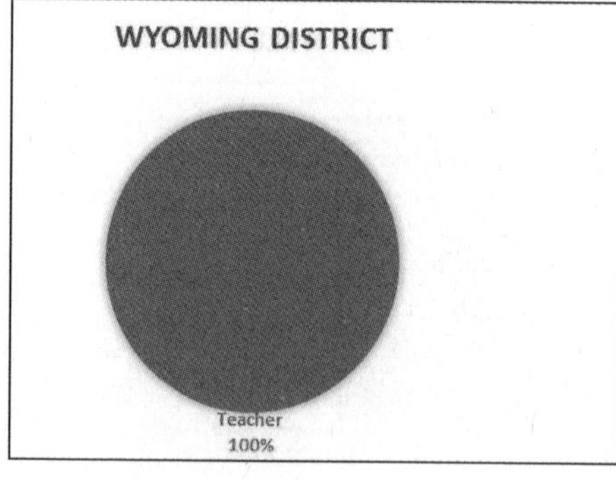

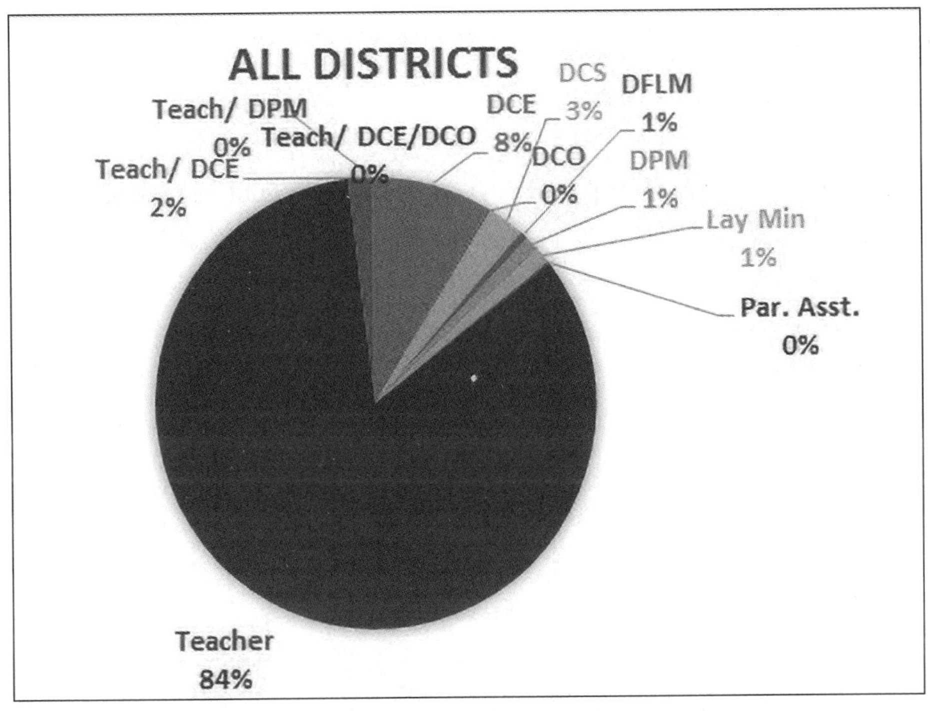

*Figures below 1% may be listed as 0%.

Bibliography

Beck, Nestor. *The Doctrine of Faith*. St. Louis: Concordia Publishing House, 1987.

Beck, Walter Herman. *Lutheran Elementary Schools in the United States*. St. Louis: Concordia Publishing House, 1939.

Behnken, John William. *This I Recall*. St. Louis: Concordia Publishing House, 1964.

Biel, Kurt W. "Parish Administration." In *The Pastor at Work*, edited by Richard R. Caemmerer, 352–73. St. Louis: Concordia Publishing House, 1960.

Braun, Mark E. "The Reception of Walther's Theology in the Wisconsin Synod." *Concordia Theological Quarterly* 77, no. 1-2 (January/April 2013): 101–39.

Bray, Gerald Lewis, and Thomas Clark Oden. *1–2 Corinthians*. Downers Grove, Ill: InterVarsity Press, 2012.

Bretscher, Paul M., August C. Stellhorn, and Arnold C. Mueller. *The Office of the Teacher in The Lutheran Church—Missouri Synod: A brief prepared for Rev. F. A. Hertwig, and Supt. S. J. Roth, September 21, 1949*. St. Louis: Concordia Historical Institute, 1949. Board for Parish Education Files: Box 16. File 11.

Brockopp, Gene W. *The Parish Role of the Lutheran Teacher*. River Forest, IL: Lutheran Education Association, 1961.

Brueggemann, H. G. "The Public Ministry in the Apostolic Age." *Concordia Theological Monthly* 22, no. 2, (February 1951): 81–109.

Brug, John F. *The Ministry of the Word*. Milwaukee, WI: Northwestern Publishing House, 2009.

Brunner, Peter. "The Ministry and the Ministry of Women." In *Women Pastors?*, edited by Matthew C. Harrison and John T. Pless, 263–94. St. Louis: Concordia Publishing House, 2012.

Calvin, John. *The Acts of the Apostles*. Translated by John W. Fraser and W. J. G. McDonald. Edited by David W. Torrance and Thomas F. Torrance. Grand Rapids, MI: William B. Eerdmans Pub. Co., 1995.

Chemnitz, Martin. *Examination of the Council of Trent: Part II*. Translated by Fred Kramer. St. Louis: Concordia Publishing House, 1979.

Chemnitz, Martin. *Loci Theologici*. Translated by J. A. O. Preus. St. Louis: Concordia Publishing House, 1989.

Chemnitz, Martin, and Jakob Andreae. *Church Order for Braunschweig-Wolfenbüttel*. (Chemnitz's Works, vol. 9.) St. Louis: Concordia Publishing House, 2015.

Chytraeus, David. *On Sacrifice.* Translated by John Warwick Montgomery. St. Louis: Concordia Publishing House, 1962.

Commission on Theology and Church Relations. *The Ministry: Offices, Procedures and Nomenclature.* St. Louis: The Lutheran Church—Missouri Synod, 1981.

Commission on Theology and Church Relations. *The Royal Priesthood: Identity and Mission.* St. Louis: The Lutheran Church—Missouri Synod, 2018.

Commission on Theology and Church Relations. *Theology and Practice of the Lord's Supper.* St. Louis: The Lutheran Church—Missouri Synod, 1983.

Concordia: The Lutheran Confessions, 2nd ed. St. Louis: Concordia Publishing House, 2009.

Concordia University Irvine. "Director of Christian Education (DCE) Program." Accessed July 31, 2018. www.cui.edu/dce.

Concordia University Irvine. "Director of Parish Music (DPM) Program." Accessed July 31, 2018. www.cui.edu/dpm.

Dallman, William, and W. H. T. Dau. *Walther and the Church.* St. Louis: Concordia Publishing House, 1938.

Engelder, Theodore Edward William, William F. Arndt, Theodore Graebner, and F. E. Mayer. *Popular Symbolics: The Doctrines of the Churches of Christendom and of Other Religious Bodies in the Light of Scripture.* St. Louis: Concordia Publishing House, 1934.

Farrell, Warren, and John Gray. *The Boy Crisis.* Dallas, TX: BenBella Books, Inc. 2018.

Fee, Gordon D., and Douglas Stuart. *How to Read the Bible for All Its Worth.* Grand Rapids, MI: Zondervan Publishing House, 2009.

Freitag, Alfred J. *"Ministers of Christ" The Office of the Lutheran Teaching Ministry. Presented at the California-Nevada District Teachers Conference. November 25–27, 1957.* St. Louis: Concordia Historical Institute, 1957. Board for Parish Education Files: Box 52. File 7.

Gallmeier, Michelle. "The Diaconate: A Misunderstood Office." *Logia,* 7, no. 3 (Holy Trinity, 1997): 23–26.

Gärtner, Bertil. "Didaskalos: The Office, Man, and Woman in the New Testament." In *Women Pastors?,* edited by Matthew C. Harrison and John T. Pless, 17–34. St. Louis: Concordia Publishing House, 2012.

Gerhard, Johann. *On the Ministry I—Theological Commonplaces.* Translated by

R. J. Dinda. Edited by B. T. G. Mayes. St. Louis: Concordia Publishing House, 2011.

Gerhard, Johann. *On the Ministry II—Theological Commonplaces.* Translated by R. J. Dinda. Edited by B. T. G. Mayes and H. R. Curtis. St. Louis: Concordia Publishing House, 2012.

Grant, Robert M., and Holt H Graham. *The Apostolic Fathers: First and Second Clement Vol. 2.* New York: Thomas Nelson & Sons, 1965.

Harrisville, Roy A. "Ministry in the New Testament." In *Called and Ordained: Lutheran Perspectives on the Office of the Ministry,* edited by Todd W. Nichol and Marc Kolden, 3–23. Minneapolis: Fortress Press, 1990.

Jamieson, Robert, A. R. Fausset, and David Brown. *Commentary Critical and Explanatory on the Whole Bible.* Oak Harbor, WA: Logos Research Systems, Inc., 1997.

Jeffcoat, James R., Jr. "Martin Luther's Doctrine of Ministry." PhD diss. Drew University, 1989.

Johnson, Daniel S. "The Ministry and the Schoolmaster: The Relation and Distinction between the Offices of Pastor and Teacher in the Missouri Synod." *Logia* 6, no. 3 (Holy Trinity 1997): 13–22.

Kähler, E. W. "Does a Congregation Ordinarily Have the Right Temporarily to Commit an Essential Part of the Holy Preaching Office to a Layman." Translated by Mark Nispel, *Logia* 6, no. 3 (Holy Trinity 1997): 37–46.

Klug, Eugene F. *Church and Ministry: The Role of Church, Pastor, and People from Luther to Walther*. St. Louis: Concordia Publishing House, 1993.

Klug, Eugene F. "Luther on the Ministry." *Concordia Theological Quarterly* 47, no. 4 (October 1983): 293–304.

Koehler, Edward W. A. *A Summary of Christian Doctrine: A Popular Presentation of the Teachings of the Bible* (2nd ed.). St. Louis: Concordia Publishing House, 2002.

Kolb, Robert A. *Christian Faith: A Lutheran Exposition*. St. Louis: Concordia Publishing House, 2013.

Kolb, Robert, and Charles P. Arand. *The Way of Concord: From Historic Text to Contemporary Witness*. St. Louis: Concordia Seminary Press, 2017.

Kowert, Henry. Letter to A. C. Stellhorn dated November 29, 1930. St. Louis: Concordia Historical Institute, 1930. Board for Parish Education Files: Box 2. File 7.

Kretzmann, Paul E. *A Brief History of Education*. St. Louis: Concordia Publishing House, 1920.

Kretzmann, Paul E. "Apostolate, Preaching Ministry, Pastorate, Synodical Office." *Concordia Journal* 15 no. 3 (July 1989): 262–73.

Kretzmann, Paul E. "Reviving a False Position with Regard to the Doctrine of the Call." St. Louis: Concordia Historical Institute, 1950. Board for Parish Education Files: Box 52. File 5.

Kretzmann, Paul E. "The Doctrine of the Call with Special Reference to the Auxiliary Offices of the Church." Paper presented at the Arlington Convention of the Northern Nebraska District of the Missouri Synod, August 20–24, 1934.

Krodel, Gerhard A. *Acts*. Minneapolis: Augsburg Publishing House, 1986.

Laetsch, Theodore F. K., ed. *The Abiding Word* (*Vol. 1*). St. Louis: Concordia Publishing House, 1946.

Laetsch, Theodore F. K., ed. *The Abiding Word* (*Vol. 2*). St. Louis: Concordia Publishing House, 1947.

Lehenbauer, Joel. *Equipping the Saints: The Intersection of the Priesthood of All Believers and the Public Ministry*. Presented at the Heartland DCE Conference at Concordia University Nebraska, May 18, 2018.

Lenski, Richard C. H. *The Interpretation of the Acts of the Apostles*. Minneapolis: Augsburg Publishing House, 1961.

Lindsay, Thomas M. *The Church and the Ministry in the Early Centuries*. New York: A. C. Armstrong and Son, 1902.

Lockwood, Gregory J. *Concordia Popular Commentary: 1 Corinthians*. St. Louis: Concordia Publishing House, 2010.

Luther, Martin. *Church and Ministry II*. Edited by Conrad Bergendoff and Helmut T. Lehmann. Vol. 40, *Luther's Works*, American Edition. Philadelphia: Fortress Press, 1958.

Luther, Martin. *Genesis: Chapters 31–37*. Translated by Paul D. Paul. Edited by Jaroslav Pelikan and Hilton C. Oswald. Vol. 6, *Luther's Works*, American Edition. St. Louis: Concordia Publishing House, 1970.

Luther, Martin. *Selected Psalms II*. Edited by Jaroslav Pelikan, Hilton C. Oswald, and Helmut T. Lehmann, Vol. 13, *Luther's Works*, American Edition. St. Louis: Concordia Publishing House, 1956.

Luther, Martin. *The Catholic Epistles*. Edited by Jaroslav Pelikan and Walter A. Hansen. Vol. 30, *Luther's Works*, American Edition. St. Louis: Concordia Publishing House, 1967.

Luther, Martin. *Word and Sacrament II.* Edited by Abdel Ross Wentz and Helmut T. Lehmann. Vol. 36, *Luther's Works,* American Edition. Philadelphia: Fortress Press, 1959.

Lutheran Church—Missouri Synod, The. *Handbook of The Lutheran Church—Missouri Synod.* St. Louis: Concordia Publishing House, 2016.

Marquart, Kurt E. *The Church and Her Fellowship, Ministry, and Governance (2nd ed.).* Fort Wayne, IN: International Foundation for Lutheran Confessional Research, 1990.

Martin, Francis, Evan Smith, and Thomas C. Oden. *Acts.* Downers Grove, IL: Inter-Varsity Press, 2006.

Mayes, Robert. "'Equipping the Saints'?: Why Ephesians 4:11–12 Opposes the Theology and Practice of Lay Ministry." *Logia* 24, no. 4 (October 2015): 7–15.

Mennicke, A. T. "The task force II recommendations." *The Lutheran Witness* 100, no. 6 (June 1981): 22–24.

Moeller, Elmer J. "Concerning the Ministry of the Church." *Concordia Theological Monthly* 22, no. 6 (June 1951): 385–416.

Mueller, Arnold C., III. *The Facts.* St. Louis: Concordia Historical Institute, 1950b. Board for Parish Education Files: Box 16. File 11.

Mueller, Arnold C. *The Ministry of the Lutheran Teacher.* St. Louis: Concordia Publishing House, 1964.

Mueller, Arnold C. *The Office of the Ministry and the Lutheran School Teacher.* St. Louis: Concordia Historical Institute, 1961. Board for Parish Education Files: Box 52. File 6.

Mueller, Arnold C. *The Status of the Parochial School Teacher.* St. Louis: Concordia Historical Institute, 1948. Board for Parish Education Files: Box 52. File 5.

Mueller, Arnold C. *Untitled partial document.* St. Louis: Concordia Historical Institute, 1950a. Board for Parish Education Files: Box 16. File 11.

Mueller, J. Theodore. "The Significance of the Doctrine of the Church and the Ministry." *Concordia Theological Monthly* 11, no. 1 (January 1940): 19–36.

Mueller, Steven P. *Called to Believe, Teach, and Confess.* Eugene, OR: Wipf & Stock Publishers, 2005.

Nadasdy, Dean. "Vocation and Mission: The Role of the Laity in the Mission of Christ." *Lutheran Mission Matters* 24, no. 1 (January 2016): 50–58.

Nafzger, S. H. "The CTCR's Report on 'The Ministry.'" *Lutheran Education Journal* 118, no. 3 (April 1983): 132–57.

Nagel, Norman. "Externum Verbum." *Logia* 6, no. 3 (Holy Trinity 1997): 27–32.

Nagel, Norman. "Luther and the Priesthood of All Believers." *Concordia Theological Quarterly* 61, no. 4 (October 1997b): 277–98.

Nass, Thomas P. "The Revised This We Believe of the WELS on the Ministry." *Logia* 10, no. 3 (Holy Trinity 2001): 31–42.

Naumann, Cheryl D. *In the Footsteps of Phoebe: A Complete History of the Deaconess Movement in The Lutheran Church—Missouri Synod.* St. Louis: Concordia Publishing House, 2009.

Nicol, O. J. *Comments Upon: Reviving a False Position with Regard to the Doctrine of the Call, by Dr. P. E. Kretzmann.* St. Louis: Concordia Historical Institute, 1952. Board for Parish Education Files: Box 52. File 5.

Nispel, Mark. "Office and Offices: Some Basic Lutheran Philology." *Logia* 7, no. 3 (Holy Trinity 1997): 5–12.

Nispel, Mark. "Pfarramt, Geography, and the Order of the Church." *Concordia Theological Quarterly* 81, no. 3-4 (July/October 2017): 239–47.

Olson, Jeannine E. *One Ministry Many Roles: Deacons and Deaconesses through the Centuries.* St. Louis: Concordia Publishing House, 1992.

Painter, Franklin V. N. *Luther on Education.* St. Louis: Concordia Publishing House, 1889.

Pelikan, Jaroslav. *Acts.* Grand Rapids, MI: Brazos Press, 2005.

Peperkorn, Todd A. "C. F. W. Walther's Kirche und Amt and the Church Office Debate Between the Missouri and Wisconsin Synods in the Early Twentieth Century." *Concordia Theological Quarterly* 65, no. 4 (October 2001): 299–322.

Piepkorn, Arthur Carl, Michael Plekon, William S. Wiecher, and Richard John Neuhaus. *The Church: Selected Writings of Arthur Carl Piepkorn.* Vol. 1. Delhi, NY: American Lutheran Publicity Bureau, 1993.

Pieper, Francis. *Christian Dogmatics (Vol. 2).* St. Louis: Concordia Publishing House, 1953.

Pragman, James H. *Traditions of Ministry: A History of the Doctrine of the Ministry in Lutheran Theology.* St. Louis: Concordia Publishing House, 1983.

Preus, Robert D. *The Doctrine of the Call in the Confessions and Lutheran Orthodoxy.* Fort Wayne, IN: Luther Academy, 1991.

Ratke, David C. *Confession and Mission, Word and Sacrament: The Ecclesial Theology of Wilhelm Löhe.* St. Louis: Concordia Publishing House, 2001.

Rengstorf, Karl H. *Apostolate and Ministry.* Translated by P. D. Pahl. St. Louis: Concordia Publishing House, 1969.

Rogness, Michael. "The Office of Deacon in the Christian Church." In *Called and Ordained: Lutheran Perspectives on the Office of the Ministry,* edited by Todd Nichol and Marc Kolden, 151–60. Minneapolis: Augsburg Fortress Publishing, 1990.

Sasse, Herman. *We Confess: The Church.* Translated by Norman Nagel. St. Louis: Concordia Publishing House, 1986.

Scaer, David P. "The Clergy as the New Testament Ministers with a Proposal for Parochial School Teachers." *Issues in Christian Education* 27, no. 1 (Spring 1993): 6–9.

Schmidt, Stephen A. *Powerless Pedagogues*. River Forest, IL: Lutheran Education Association, 1972.

Schöne, Jobst. *The Christological Character of the Office of the Ministry and the Royal Priesthood*. Northville, SD: Logia Publishing, 1994.

Schulz, Gregory P. "Improving the Relationship between Pastor and Teacher in Light of the Doctrine of the Divine Call." DMin diss. Concordia Theological Seminary, 1992.

Schwermann, Albert H. "The Doctrine of the Call." In *The Pastor at Work,* edited by Richard R. Caemmerer, 87–124. St. Louis: Concordia Publishing House, 1960.

Sharf, Edwin. "The Call to the Public Use of the Keys." In *Our Great Heritage, vol. 3,* 496–527. Edited by Lyle W. Lange. Milwaukee, WI: Northwestern Publishing House, 1991.

Smith, Robert H. *Concordia Commentary: Acts*. St. Louis: Concordia Publishing House, 1970.

Staniforth, Maxwell. *Early Christian Writings: The Apostolic Fathers.* New York: Dorset Press, 1986.

Stellhorn, August C. *Comments Upon—Reviving a False Position with Regard to the Doctrine of the Call.* St. Louis: Concordia Historical Institute, 1962. Board for Parish Education Files: Box 52. File 5.

Stellhorn, August C. *Exemption of Teachers' College Students*. St. Louis: Concordia Historical Institute, 1942. Board for Parish Education Files: Box 54. File 15.

Stellhorn, August C. *Letter to A. W. Banke dated September 11, 1934.* St. Louis: Concordia Historical Institute, 1934. Board for Parish Education Files: Box 2. File 6.

Stellhorn, August C. *Letter to H. Hillman dated October 5, 1934*. St. Louis: Concordia Historical Institute, 1934b. Board for Parish Education Files: Box 2. File 6.

Stellhorn, August C. *Letter to J. R. Harmening dated December 30, 1930*. St. Louis: Concordia Historical Institute, 1930. Board for Parish Education Files: Box 2. File 7.

Stellhorn, August C. *Letter to Supt. S. J. Roth, October 7, 1949*. St. Louis: Concordia Historical Institute, 1949. Board for Parish Education Files: Box 16. File 11.

Stellhorn, August C. *Schools of The Lutheran Church—Missouri Synod*. St. Louis: Concordia Publishing House, 1963.

Stellhorn, August C. *Special Problem for the Board for Parish Education Meeting. September 19, 1949*. St. Louis: Concordia Historical Institute, 1949a. Board for Parish Education Files: Box 16. File 11.

Stellhorn, August C. *The Lutheran Teacher in the Ministry of the Church*. Presented at the Western District Teachers Conference, November 5–7, 1952. St. Louis: Concordia Historical Institute, 1952. Board for Parish Education Files: Box 52. File 7.

Stellhorn, August C. *The Lutheran Teacher's Position in the Ministry of the Congregation*. St. Louis: Concordia Historical Institute, n.d. Board for Parish Education Files: Box 16. File 9.

Stellhorn, August C. *Trees Diagram*. St. Louis: Concordia Historical Institute, n.d. Board for Parish Education Files: Box 52. File 5.

Stellhorn, Frederick W. *Annotations on the Acts of the Apostles*, vol. VI. Edited by H. E. Jacobs. New York: The Christian Literature Co., 1896.

Stott, John R. W. *The Spirit, the Church, and the World*. Downers Grove, IL: Inter-Varsity Press, 1990.

Suelflow, August R. *Heritage in Motion: Readings in the History of The Lutheran Church—Missouri Synod, 1962–1995*. St. Louis: Concordia Publishing House, 1998.

Sutton, A. Trevor. *Being Lutheran*. St. Louis: Concordia Publishing House, 2016.

Talbert, Charles H. *Reading Acts: A Literary and Theological Commentary on the Acts of the Apostles*. Macon, GA: Smyth & Helwys Pub., 2005.

Toepper, Robert M. "Is the Lutheran Teacher a Minister: Part I." *Lutheran Education Journal* 131, no. 2 (September/October 1995): 64–79.

Toepper, Robert M. "Is the Lutheran Teacher a Minister: Part II." *Lutheran Education Journal* 131, no. 3 (January/February 1996): 124–42.

Toepper, Robert M. "Is the Lutheran Teacher a Minister: Part III." *Lutheran Education Journal* 131, no. 5 (May/June 1996b): 249–68.

Walther, Carl F. W. *Church and Ministry: Kirche und Amt.* Translated by John T. Mueller. St. Louis: Concordia Publishing House, 1987.

Walther, Carl F. W. *Pastoral Theology.* Translated by Christian Tiews. Edited by David W. Loy. St. Louis: Concordia Publishing House, 2017.

Walther, Carl F. W. *The Church and the Office of the Ministry.* Edited by Matthew C. Harrison. St. Louis: Concordia Publishing House, 2012.

Walther, Carl F. W. *The Congregation's Right to Choose Its Pastor*. Translated by Fred Kramer. St. Louis: Concordia Seminary, 1997.

Walther, Carl F. W. *Walther and the Church*. St. Louis: Concordia Publishing House, 1938.

Walvoord, John F., and Roy B. Zuck. *The Bible Knowledge Commentary: An Exposition of the Scriptures.* Wheaton, IL: Victor Books, 1985.

Waterworth, James. *The Council of Trent: The Canons and Decrees of the Sacred and Oecumenical Council of Trent*. London: Dolman, 1848.

Wenner, G. U. "Hands, Imposition of." In *The Lutheran Cyclopedia*, edited by Erwin L. Lueker, 360. St. Louis: Concordia Publishing House, 1975.

Wiersbe, Warren W. *The Bible Exposition Commentary*. Wheaton, IL: Victor Books, 1996.

Wohlrabe, John C., Jr. "An historical analysis of the doctrine of the ministry in the Lutheran Church—Missouri Synod." ThD. diss. Concordia Seminary, St. Louis, 1987.

Ziegler, Caspar. *The Diaconate of the Ancient and Medieval Church*. Edited by Charles P. Schaum and Albert B. Collver. St. Louis: Concordia Publishing House, 2014.

Zimmerman, Paul A. "The Lutheran Teacher: Minister of the Church—Revisited." *Lutheran Education Journal* 131, no. 5 (May/June 1996): 269–75.

Index

In his dual role as both a district executive and as a university professor who teaches and equips future church workers, Dr. David Rueter is uniquely positioned to understand what it means to be a called commissioned minister in The Lutheran Church—Missouri Synod. In *Called to Serve: A Theology of Commissioned Ministry*, Rueter cogently explores this auxiliary office within the Office of Public Ministry through the lenses of church history and theology, as presented by highly recognizable church fathers (Luther, Pieper, Walther, and more), to establish and uplift the value of commissioned ministers. This text provides readers with a deep and rich exposition that supports the existence and need for Kingdom workers who are called into professional church work vocations in a non-ordained capacity.

Dr. Kevin Borchers,
associate professor of Christian education,
assistant director of DCE program,
director of colloquy at Concordia University Chicago

Commissioned ministers have had a substantial impact on many Lutherans, but their status is often the subject of significant confusion. Are they mini-pastors? super-laity? a mixture of both? Rueter tackles these questions head-on in *Called to Serve*, showing along the way that debates about commissioned ministry are nothing new. Most important, he draws on Scripture, Luther, Gerhard, and Walther to propose an understanding of commissioned ministry that honors both it and the pastoral office.

Rev. David W. Loy, PhD,
associate dean of Christ College,
director of FaithWorks Center,
associate professor at Concordia University Irvine

Dave Rueter has done an excellent job of tracing the theology and history of the offices for ministry in the LCMS. He has highlighted the conflicts as workers have sought to serve together in ministry. While professional church workers are called to serve congregations as a unified team, conflict has often disrupted this leadership. How we recognize ministers of religion ordained and commissioned in conventions of the districts and synod is an ongoing debate, which Dave addresses with a recommendation. This book is a helpful study for all levels of the Church.

Rev. Dr. Larry Stoterau,
president emeritus, Pacific Southwest District of the LCMS

David Rueter's *Called to Serve* is a much-needed revisit on the Office of Public Ministry. Thoroughly researched from the days of Luther up to the present day, Rueter reveals the lack of clarity or fogginess that commissioned ministers hold (and perhaps feel) in regard to their place or position within a congregation. Perhaps because of Rueter's own family background and vocation as a commissioned minister, one can absorb not only the research expertise he brings to this topic but his passion too. In his closing chapter, Rueter provides his own take on auxiliary ministries and the Office of the Public Ministry. The book is well-researched and succinctly written and organized. The chapters and sub-headings make the work easy to navigate and enjoyable to read. After consuming the work, I not only felt more well-versed in the Office of Public Ministry but honored to be a part of it. *Called to Serve* is both informative and inspirational.

Dr. James Pingel,
dean of the School of Education,
Concordia University Wisconsin